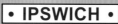

UEFA CUP WINNERS
1980/81
40TH ANNIVERSARY

Written by Brian Leng
Statistics compiled by Chris Leng

a twocan publication

©2020. Published by twocan under licence from Ipswich Town FC.

ISBN 978-1-913362-73-7

PICTURES:
Action Images, East Anglian Daily Times, Press Association & Ipswich Town FC.

THE DAWN OF THE ROBSON ERA...

CHAIRMAN JOHN COBBOLD
WELCOMES BOBBY TO THE CLUB

...AND WITH FULHAM

BOBBY ROBSON TRAINING WITH ENGLAND

To trace the origins of Ipswich Town's 1981 UEFA Cup success, you would need to turn the clock back a further twelve years, to 13th January 1969 to be precise, the day that Bobby Robson took over the manager's hot-seat at Portman Road. For it was Robson who turned the middle- of-the-road Suffolk club into one that stood toe to toe withthe finest clubs, not only in the English game, but also in Europe throughout the seventies and early eighties.

As a player, Bobby Robson had enjoyed a hugely successful career as a talented wing-half with first Fulham and then West Bromwich Albion, as well as picking up 20 full international caps for England along the way. After a second spell at Craven Cottage towards the end of his playing career he was given his first chance in football management with the London club, but after failing to keep the club in the top flight in his first season in charge, he discovered he had lost his job when he was travelling home from training and spotted the headline 'Robson sacked' on the Evening Standard billboard outside Putney Station. He later recalled after returning to Craven Cottage to clear his desk, walking out onto the Craven Cottage pitch and standing in tears in the centre circle, after taking one last look at the ground where he began his playing career almost twenty years earlier. At that moment, with his hopes of a career in football management seemingly in tatters, it would have been almost impossible to imagine that Bobby Robson would go on to become one of the greatest managers ever produced by the English game and one who would ultimately receive a knighthood for his services to football.

Ironically, on that very same day, the Ipswich Town boss Bill McGarry announced that he was leaving the club after agreeing to take over as manager of Wolverhampton Wanderers. Perhaps what is not so widely known is that the subsequent appointment of Bobby Robson as his successor almost didn't materialise at all with the Portman Road board targeting first Frank O'Farrell at Torquay United and then former Irish international Billy Bingham. Both, it was reported, had been offered the job, but when they declined, the Town board turned their attention to Robson who had been recommended by Chelsea boss Dave Sexton, a man apparently held in high regard by the Portman Road hierarchy.

The interview took place in the Great Eastern Hotel in London and his appointment was confirmed in a statement by chairman John Cobbold which read...

'We were vastly impressed with Mr Robson and there was no doubt in our minds that he was the man for the job. He is obviously pretty tough, but most pleasant and his whole life is bound up with football. We have not given him a contract, but I realise no manager can be judged in less than two years. I sincerely hope Bobby stays considerably longer than that.'

For his part, the new manager quickly made his managerial philosophy abundantly clear when he announced at his first press conference: 'I've come here because I know, from my own personal point of view, that as far as my own working conditions are concerned, this is a club that will allow me to manage and are prepared to give me a chance.' Having total control of a club was exactly the sort of job Robson had been looking for, although in those early days one or two of the more senior players certainly didn't embrace his ideas on how the game should be played.

In particular, Tommy Carroll and club captain Bill Baxter were constantly in conflict with their new boss and as Robson recalled in his autobiography 'Farewell but not Goodbye', matters came to a head in February 1971 when Carroll and Town's new boss exchanged blows in a massive dressing-room bust up. As a result, Carroll asked for a showdown meeting with John Cobbold and with Robson in attendance, the club chairman made it abundantly clear that he had no time for player power at his club, stating...

'So, Tommy, I understand you want to see me, well here I am and have a good look at me. Now, there's the manager over there, he runs the club so talk to him. Now I'm sodding off!'

The significance of the meeting cannot be overstated as it gave Bobby Robson total control at Portman Road and never again would his authority be challenged by one of his players or anyone else at the club for that matter. Robson later recalled: 'I'm not proud of how events unfolded, but it was a battle I just had to win.' Predictably, the days of Baxter and Carroll were now numbered and both were soon moved on to new clubs, Carroll joining Birmingham City and Baxter moving to Hull City. As a result, Robson immediately appointed Mick Mills as club captain, a player who would skipper the side throughout the Bobby Robson era at Portman Road and one who would eventually make a record number of appearances for the club.

As John Cobbold had rightly predicted, it would be at least two years before Robson would begin to stamp his mark on the club and, at times, those early years were certainly less than comfortable for the new Portman Road boss. On one notable occasion after a particularly bad run of results and with the supporters baying for his blood, Robson was summoned to the boardroom. Fully expecting the worst, he was astounded when John Cobbold apologised to him for the behaviour of the fans and assured him he had the whole-hearted support of the board. It was a moment that Bobby Robson never forgot and when his reputation in the game soared in the years ahead, he turned down approaches from a number of high-profile clubs in the English game, preferring instead to remain loyal in recognition of the support the chairman and directors had given him at the start of his managerial career at Portman Road.

BILL BAXTER

MICK MILLS

CLUB CAPTAIN THROUGHOUT THE ENTIRE ROBSON ERA

1978
FA CUP
WINNERS

BOBBY ROBSON AND HIS COACHING STAFF WITH THE TEXACO CUP

KEVIN BEATTIE

in his third full season in charge, they finished a commendable fourth place in Division One bringing European football to Portman Road for the first time since the heady days of Alf Ramsey in the early '60s.

The new manager had introduced a policy of operating shrewdly in the transfer market and, perhaps more importantly, developing a scouting system that would soon become a production line of talented youngsters who would eventually become the backbone of the 1981 UEFA Cup winning side. The net was spread far and wide and the array of talent that this network unearthed was truly amazing. Kevin Beattie and Steve McCall were spotted in Carlisle, John Wark, Alan Brazil and George Burley in Scotland and Eric Gates in the north east with the future central defensive partnership of Russell Osman and Terry Butcher also coming through the ranks.

These and many other talented youngsters were developed under the watchful eye of youth team coach Bobby Ferguson, a man who would eventually become Bobby Robson's right-hand man and a key figure in the 1981 UEFA Cup success. The first signs of the bright future that lay ahead came in 1973 when Town lifted the FA Youth Cup, a feat they repeated two years later.

Perhaps it should be mentioned that a young Paul Gascoigne was also given a trial at Portman Road during this period, but after failing to impress, was sent back home to Gateshead. Few could have predicted that in the years ahead, he and Bobby Robson would team up as player and manager on the very highest stage of international football.

When Robson did need to move into the transfer market, his buys were invariably great business for the club with, Paul Mariner, Arnold Mühren and Franz Thijssen all giving outstanding service during their time at club. One of Robson's best buys and one he was always proud of was 'keeper Paul Cooper who was picked up for a modest fee of only £23,000 from Birmingham City.

Throughout the 1970s, Ipswich Town were rarely outside of the top six in Division One playing a style of full-blooded attacking football that Portman Road fans hadn't witnessed for years. The Texaco Cup was won in 1973 with a memorable two-legged victory over arch rivals Norwich City, and five years later they went one better to lift the FA Cup, Roger Osborne netting the only goal of the game to secure victory over Arsenal.

The league title however was proving to be an elusive prize and when the 1980/81 season dawned, few could have predicted that the campaign would extend to an incredible 66 games as Bobby Robson's side chased an unprecedented treble.

Of all the players bought by Bobby Robson during his thirteen years with Ipswich Town, it is doubtful whether any player represented better value for money than goalkeeper Paul Cooper. Signed from Birmingham City in June 1974 for a modest £23,000 fee, the powerfully-built 'keeper went on to become something of a Blues legend playing an impressive 575 first-team games for the club.

Paul actually began his playing career in non-league football as a striker, but soon began to show potential as a goalkeeper, prompting Birmingham City to offer him apprenticeship terms in June 1971. At St. Andrews he soon became an understudy to regular 'keeper Dave Latchford and made his first-team debut seven months later in a 6-3 victory over Portsmouth. Thereafter however, his appearances were somewhat sporadic and when Birmingham signed Welsh international Gary Sprake from Leeds United for £100,000, a world record for a goalkeeper at the time, it was obvious his first-team opportunities would be fairly limited.

In March 1974, Bobby Robson persuaded Paul to join Ipswich on loan as cover for Laurie Sivell, but after impressing in reserve team football, the transfer was made permanent a few months later. His breakthrough came early in the 1975/76 season when, after Ipswich lost their first home match 3-0 to Newcastle United, he was drafted into the first team where he remained for the rest of the season. Thereafter, Paul pretty much held the 'keeper's jersey for the rest of his career at Portman Road earning a reputation as one of the best 'keepers in the English game and also something of an expert at saving penalties. A great student of the game, he would study footage of opposition penalty takers and keep a mental dossier on each player, a technique that produced staggering results. In the 1978/79 season he saved five out of the seven penalties he faced and the following campaign was even better when he saved eight out of ten, a league record at the time.

Having helped Town lift the FA Cup in 1978, Paul played in all but one of the games in the 1980/81 UEFA Cup success and in the final against AZ Alkmaar he produced a Man of the Match performance to keep the Dutch side at bay and ensure his team lifted the trophy. It had been a magnificent campaign for the man the Ipswich fans nicknamed 'Super Cooper' and it came as no surprise when they voted him their Player of the Season.

Despite being widely regarded as one of the finest 'keepers in the English game, Paul was never honoured at international level. One of the last players from the Bobby Robson era, he continued as Town's first choice goalkeeper until June 1987 when he was given a free transfer and was immediately signed by former Ipswich colleague Bryan Hamilton who was now manager of Leicester City. There followed spells with Manchester City and Stockport County before he retired from the top-class game at the end of the 1990/91 season. One of the All-Time Greats at Portman Road, Paul was inducted into the Ipswich Town Hall of Fame in 2014.

PAUL
Cooper

PLAYER PROFILE

DATE OF BIRTH:	21 December 1953
PLACE OF BIRTH:	Cannock, Staffordshire
IPSWICH TOWN:	575 Appearances
1980/81 UEFA CUP:	11 Appearances

IPSWICH TOWN 5
Wark (13 Pen, 15, 29 Pen, 79 Pen), Mariner (61)

ARIS SALONIKA 1
Pallas (48 Pen)

Wednesday 17 September 1980
Portman Road · Attendance: 20,842

IPSWICH TOWN:

PAUL COOPER · GEORGE BURLEY · MICK MILLS · FRANS THIJSSEN
RUSSELL OSMAN · TERRY BUTCHER · JOHN WARK · ARNOLD MÜHREN
PAUL MARINER · ALAN BRAZIL · ERIC GATES
SUBS USED: KEVIN BEATTIE · KEVIN O'CALLAGHAN

ARIS SALONIKA:

GIORGOS PANTZIARAS · THALIS TSIRIMOKOS · GIANNIS VENOS
THEODOROS PALLAS · KOSTAS MOKALIS · GIORGOS FOIROS
GIORGOS ZINDROS · GIORGOS SEMERTZIDIS · DINOS KOUIS
KOSTAS BALLIS · THEODOROS ZELILIDIS
SUB USED: KOSTAS DRAMBIS

REFEREE: ANTÓNIO GARRIDO (PORTUGAL)

UEFA CUP WINNERS
1980/81
40TH ANNIVERSARY

TOWN·F·C

1st
ROUND
FIRST LEG

Having finished in third place in Division One the season before, Bobby Robson's side continued their fine form into the 1980/81 league campaign, winning five of their first six matches before turning their attention to the UEFA Cup. To lift the trophy Ipswich would need to safely negotiate six two-legged ties in a competition that included some of the top sides in European football and well as one or two less familiar names.

The draw had paired them with Aris Salonika, who were something of an unknown quantity to the Ipswich players apart from John Wark who ironically, just a year earlier, had been approached by the Greek side with an offer to join their club.

John explains: "My mother-in-law comes from a small town near Salonika and I went out there with my wife Toula for a month's holiday during the 1979 close season. The local press got to hear I was in town and came down to interview me, after which my wife and I set off for a walk on the beach only to be approached by two very official looking men, both smartly dressed and carrying briefcases. They introduced themselves as Aris Salonika officials and asked if I would be interested in playing for them. I was a bit taken aback and explained to them that I was under contract to Ipswich and even if I did want to move, which I didn't, it would be impossible."

Knowing little about the Greek side, Bobby Robson decided to travel to Greece and run the rule over Town's opponents. In his programme notes the Ipswich manager said...

'Starting out in Europe is always an exciting part of any season. First there is the draw and then the build up to the first round games when players and supporters alike are both keyed up. There is always the likelihood, of course, that we will be drawn against a side about whom we know very little and Aris Salonika are a classic example. We always try to do our homework, however, and with this in mind I flew out to Greece at the weekend to watch them in action. Looking through the other sides in the competition it is obvious how difficult it is going to be to keep progressing. But we have a European pedigree ourselves and a lot of sides will be hoping they don't come up against Ipswich. Our supporters can play a big part in helping us overcome each hurdle, starting tonight. In Europe, for example, we can expect to meet sides with fiercely partisan crowds who are almost worth a goal start.'

Bobby Robson could hardly have imagined how prophetic those words would be as Town's first round tie with the Greek side developed into a torrid affair, particularly in the second leg as his team came within a whisker of falling at the first hurdle.

SKIPPER MICK MILLS SHAKES HANDS WITH THE ARIS SALONIKA CAPTAIN

THE JOURNEY BEGINS...

JOHN WARK SENDS ARIS GOALKEEPER PANTZIARAS THE WRONG WAY WITH HIS SECOND PENALTY

Bobby Robson was able to field a full-strength team for this game with Paul Mariner and Eric Gates both returning to the fold after helping England to a 4-0 win over Norway in a World Cup Qualifier at Wembley. Mariner had capped a great performance by netting one of the goals, but it was also a special night for Eric Gates who picked up his first full international cap for his country.

Having been drawn at home for the first leg, Town were looking to secure a decent advantage to take to Greece for the second leg, but they could hardly have imagined achieving such an emphatic victory in a one-sided game that wasn't without controversy.

The home side were in control from the off and after only 13 minutes they opened the scoring after Gates was upended in the box and referee Garrido immediately pointed to the spot. Despite the furious protests of the Greek side, Wark kept his cool and slotted a right-foot shot high into the net giving the 'keeper no chance. Two minutes later, Town doubled their advantage and again it was Wark on target, firing home from just inside the box when Mills left-wing corner was punched clear by the Aris Salonika 'keeper.

Then on 29 minutes, the home side were awarded another penalty, and again it was Gates who was brought to the ground after turning his man just inside the box. Predictably, mass protests followed, but unperturbed Wark sent the 'keeper the wrong way to complete his hat-trick. Some of the tactics employed by the Greek side were crude in the extreme and on 35 minutes a horrendous challenge on Gates resulted in Foiros being show a red card.

It had been a miserable first period for the visitors who were in danger of completely losing control, but they were presented with a way back into the game when Butcher was adjudged to have brought down Zindros in the box. Pallas stepped up to take the kick and slotted the ball home despite a brave effort to save by Cooper. Soon afterwards the home side should have increased their lead when a cross from Mühren found Mariner unmarked in the box, but the Ipswich striker saw his chip over the 'keeper drop agonisingly over the bar. However, he made amends a few minutes later with a stinging right-foot volley low into the corner of the net from just inside the area to restore Town's three goal advantage. Amazingly, with only eleven minutes remaining, the home side were awarded another penalty for yet another foul on Gates and again Wark stepped up to fire the spot kick high into the net, the Greek 'keeper again being sent the wrong way. An emphatic 5-1 victory was more than many fans could have hoped for and for Man of the Match John Wark, it was a truly amazing night - four goals including a hat-trick of penalties which, ironically, were all awarded for fouls on Eric Gates.

In his post-match press conference Bobby Robson pulled no punches in his criticism of the tactics employed by the Greek side, warning that despite the 5-1 scoreline, nothing was being taking for granted...

'Anything can happen, they'll turn the game of football into a type of war with their tackling and intimidation and the way they can bring a match down. I can't control what they can do, but I can control our attitude and the way we behave and the way we will play our game. Strict discipline is required and we must walk away from things that will undoubtedly go on out there. If we just get on with it, play a sporting but tough British style of football, we should get out of it all right.'

Arguably the most prolific goalscoring midfielder of his generation, John Wark was an outstanding performer throughout Ipswich Town's 1980/81 UEFA Cup campaign scoring no fewer than 14 goals, which equalled the all-time competition record. Ironically, John was never deployed as a striker and was used by Bobby Robson as a holding midfielder alongside Arnold Mühren and Frans Thijssen, however, his terrific energy allowed him to make box-to-box runs that produced goals to devastating effect.

Born in Glasgow, John was spotted by Ipswich scouts while playing for Drumchapel Amateurs when he was only 15 years old and signed schoolboy terms for Town in 1972 after turning down overtures from a number of clubs including Scottish giants Celtic. His first-team debut came in March 1975 when, playing as a central-defender, he helped Town secure a memorable 3-2 FA Cup Sixth round second replay victory over Leeds United at Filbert Street, Leicester. However, it was the 1976/77 season before he finally became established as a first-team regular and in June 1977, having already been capped by Scotland at Under-21 level, John was selected for the full squad only to miss out following a hamstring injury sustained in pre-season training.

The following season, he was a key member of the Ipswich team that lifted the FA Cup for the first time in the club's history with an unforgettable 1-0 victory over Arsenal at Wembley. John produced a great performance in the final, hitting the woodwork twice with long-range efforts before Roger Osborne's goal finally ensured the coveted trophy would be heading to Suffolk. Full international honours finally arrived in May 1979 when he was selected to play for Scotland against Wales at Ninian Park in the British Home International Championship, the first of 29 caps he would win for his country, including three in the 1982 World Cup in Spain.

The 1980/81 season was undoubtedly the finest of John's Ipswich Town career and apart from his goalscoring exploits in the UEFA Cup, he finished the campaign with 22 league and cup goals on the domestic scene and was named the PFA's 'Player of the Year'. In addition, he picked up the 'Bravo Award', an annual award by the Italian magazine Guerin Sportivo to European football's most outstanding young player. The summer of 1980 also saw John and some of his Ipswich colleagues hit the big screen when they were invited to team up with Pele and Bobby Moore in the making of the cult film 'Escape to Victory' starring Michael Caine and Sylvester Stallone.

John left Ipswich to join Liverpool in a £450,000 deal in 1984 and at Anfield he fulfilled his dream of winning the First Division Championship before returning to Portman Road four years later. Then, following a spell with Middlesbrough, he returned to Ipswich for a third time before finally hanging up his boots in November 1996 at the age of 39. In all, John made 678 appearances for the club, a record only bettered by Mick Mills, and during his Town career he picked up the supporters' 'Player of the Year' award no fewer than four times. In 2007 he was inducted into Ipswich Town's 'Hall of Fame' and continues to be very much involved on the Portman Road scene in a variety of roles and currently works in match-day hospitality.

WARK HUGS ROGER OSBORNE AFTER HIS FA CUP FINAL WINNER

WARK V NEW ZEALAND, 1982 FIFA WORLD CUP

JOHN Wark

PLAYER PROFILE

DATE OF BIRTH:	4 August 1957
PLACE OF BIRTH:	Glasgow
IPSWICH TOWN:	679 Appearances · 179 goals
1980/81 UEFA CUP:	12 Appearances · 14 goals

ARIS SALONIKA 3
Tsirimokos (4), Drambis (22, 65)

IPSWICH TOWN 1
Gates (75)

Wednesday 1 October 1980
Kaftanzoglio Stadium · Attendance: 40,000

ARIS SALONIKA:
GIORGOS PANTZIARAS · GIANNIS VENOS · THALIS TSIRIMOKOS
KOSTAS MOKALIS · GIANNIS MICHALITSOS · KOSTAS DRAMBIS
KOSTAS BALLIS · GIORGOS SEMERTZIDIS · DINOS KOUIS
NIKOS CHATZIANTONIOU · THEODOROS ZELILIDIS
SUBS USED: TASOS ZELIDIS · THEMISTOKLIS VAGGIS

IPSWICH TOWN:
PAUL COOPER · GEORGE BURLEY · MICK MILLS · FRANS THIJSSEN
RUSSELL OSMAN · TERRY BUTCHER · JOHN WARK · ARNOLD MÜHREN
PAUL MARINER · ALAN BRAZIL · ERIC GATES
SUBS USED: KEVIN BEATTIE · STEVE McCALL

REFEREE: ALOJZY JARGUS (POLAND)

**UEFA CUP WINNERS
1980/81
40TH ANNIVERSARY**

1st
ROUND
SECOND LEG

Despite Bobby Robson's words of caution, the vast majority of supporters could have been forgiven for thinking the tie was effectively over after the 5-1 first-leg victory at Portman Road, but from the moment the Ipswich party touched down on Greek soil, it was pretty obvious this was going to be anything but an easy ride.

The game was staged in Greek bandit country and the emotions of the Greek fans, volatile at the best of times, had been stirred by rumours that Ipswich had bribed the referee in the first leg, hence the award of three penalties. These rumours were absolute nonsense of course, but were swallowed hook, line and sinker by the home fans prompting the authorities to order an armed police escort for the Ipswich party. Then, the day before the game, one newspaper carried the headline: 'Tomorrow You Die!' and by the time Mick Mills led out his team the following night, the vast majority of the 40,000 crowd packed into the Kaftanzoglio Stadium were baying for English blood.

As Paul Mariner set the game under way, fire-crackers were exploding on the terraces prompting a desperate appeal over the PA system begging fans not to set fire to the stadium. In such a hostile atmosphere, it was vital that Robson's team kept their composure, but they could not have got off to a worse start, conceding with only four minutes on the clock.

The goal came from an in-swinging right-wing corner which was met at the far post by Tsirimokos whose effort was cleared by the Ipswich defence only for the officials to rule that the ball had crossed the line. Buoyed by their early success and roared on by their fanatical fans, the home side pressed forward at every opportunity as Bobby Robson's team struggled to find their rhythm.

The game was developing into a scrappy encounter with very little flowing football probably due, in part at least, to the terrible state of the pitch which was bumpy and concrete-hard. Nevertheless, it was a piece of pure quality that saw the Greek side double their advantage on 22 minutes. There seemed to be little danger when the ball was played up to Drambis on the edge of the box, but he turned brilliantly to unleash a terrific right-foot volley that flew in the corner of the net with Cooper well beaten. Suddenly it was 'game on' and as the dejected Ipswich players trooped off at half time, they knew they faced a real battle in the second period to stay in the competition.

The second half began with Aris Salonika enjoying the lion's share of possession without threatening the Ipswich goal, but little was seen of the visitor's crisp, attacking play that had been the feature of their emphatic Portman Road victory. However, in a rare breakaway they were awarded a free-kick 25 yards from goal and when the ball was played in it found it's way to Mariner racing in behind the home defence, but his effort was straight at the 'keeper who was injured as the two players collided.

ERIC GATES

Reflecting on both the ties and arguably the most important goal of his Ipswich Town career, Eric Gates said...

'**It was really worrying to be so close to losing our four-goal advantage from the first game. Fifteen minutes into the second half, when it was 2-0 to them, I was confident we could hang on. Then when they scored their third, I thought we'd had it. I've never been more relieved to see the ball hit the back of the net.**

I haven't really got any pleasant memories of Greece. The pitch was a disgrace and their players were up to all sorts of tricks, shirt-pulling, nipping and spitting. A lot of people think we were lucky to get three penalties in the first game, but in my book the referee was right each time. Funnily enough, although the Greeks were very physical in that match, they conceded penalties because there tackles were just plain clumsy, rather than vicious.'

Then Brazil went on a surging run through the middle to send in a rasping shot which the home 'keeper couldn't hold but the ball was cleared for a corner before the oncoming Mariner could get the vital touch.

At this stage, the game was evenly balanced with the visitors carving out the best chances, but on 60 minutes Kouis had a great chance only to head over the bar from eight yards when the ball was crossed in from the right. Then on 65 minutes, the pendulum swung dramatically towards an Aris Salonika victory when Drambis netted his second strike of the game to send the home fans into delirium. The goal came from a right-wing corner and when the ball was headed back into the box, the midfielder managed to get in front of Cooper to send a looping header goalwards. Mills, standing on the line, managed to it hook clear only for the referee to again rule that the ball had crossed the line. What seemed inconceivable at the start was now becoming a reality - one more goal from the home side and Bobby Robson's side would exit the competition courtesy of the away goals rule.

If ever Robson's team needed resolve and determination then this was the moment. The atmosphere in the stadium was now at fever pitch as the Greek side pressed forward looking for the goal that would see them through and on 69 minutes they almost got it, Kouis heading a right-wing corner narrowly wide with Cooper at full stretch. Then the play switched to the opposite end with Mariner winning the ball on the right and when he crossed into the goalmouth, two goal-bound efforts were blocked by Pantziaras before he finally managed to smother the ball just short of the line.

Little had been seen of Eric Gates as a goalscoring threat, but with 15 minutes remaining he netted a priceless goal to turn the tie firmly back in Town's favour. The goal came from a long clearance by Cooper, headed down to Mühren by Brazil. The Dutchman turned inside before playing the ball to Gates on the edge of the box who rifled a brilliant first time shot low into the corner of the net giving the home 'keeper no chance.

It was a moment of fitting revenge for the Ipswich striker who throughout the two legs had been the subject of more than his share of the underhand tactics employed by the Greek side. The stadium, which had been really bouncing seconds earlier, suddenly fell silent apart from the joyous celebrations of the two hundred or so Ipswich fans who had made the long journey out to Greece. Meanwhile on the bench, Bobby Robson immediately changed to a more defensive formation sending on Steve McCall in place of Alan Brazil and soon afterwards Kevin Beattie entered the fray as Ipswich comfortably played out the closing minutes.

It had hardly been a classic performance by Robson's team and if they thought their troubles were over as they prepared to the leave the ground, they were in for a shock as their team coach was bombarded with rocks by angry Greek fans forcing everyone on board to dive for cover.

GEORGE BURLEY

At his peak there were few more talented forwards than Eric Gates who possessed the rare ability to destroy the opposition with his trademark turn and devastating shooting. Employed by Bobby Robson playing just behind the front two, defenders found it almost impossible to mark him out of the game and he would often create goals literally out of nothing.

Eric, whose brother Bill had played for Middlesbrough in the early 1960s, was spotted by Ipswich Town while playing in local football in the north east and joined the Portman Road ground-staff as an apprentice in July 1971. He made his senior debut a little over two years later when he came off the bench in a 2-0 victory over Wolves, but it was the 1977/78 season before he began to appear regularly in the first eleven. A regular goalscorer for the club, Eric had opened his account in the 3-0 UEFA Cup victory over Club Brugge in 1975 and many Town supporters will no doubt recall the two goals he scored to secure an epic win over Barcelona in the 1978/79 European Cup Winners' Cup.

Disappointingly, Eric missed out on a place in Town's 1978 FA Cup-winning team, but by the time the 1980/81 campaign came around, he had well and truly established himself as a first-team regular making a total of sixty appearances including all but one of the UEFA Cup games. His contribution that season was immense and few can forget his vital goal in the first round second leg against Aris Salonika when Town were in danger of surrendering their first-leg lead.

Although rarely deployed as a main striker, Eric's record of 96 goals in all competitions for Ipswich Town stands testament to his eye for goal and many of his strikes were of the truly spectacular fashion. Indeed, 'Match of the Day' viewers of his generation will no doubt recall Eric's goal against Liverpool at Anfield in February 1980, a superb volley from outside the box that stunned the Kop and was voted Goal of the Month.

International recognition finally arrived in September 1980 when Eric was selected to play for England in a 4-0 World Cup Qualifier victory over Norway at Wembley and he then held his place for their next game, a 2-1 defeat against Romania in Bucharest. Somewhat surprisingly, considering the outstanding form he was producing with Ipswich, Eric was never selected to play for his country again.

Eric's career with Town finally came to an end in 1985 when he returned to the north east to join the ill-fated Lawrie McMenemy era at Sunderland that culminated in the Roker Park club dropping into English football's third tier for the first time in their history. Nevertheless, Eric quickly became established as a key figure in Sunderland's recovery and immediate return to Division Two forming a devastating strike partnership with new signing Marco Gabbiadini which Roker fans named the 'G-Force'. The pair continued to flourish in the second tier and became a significant factor in the club's promotion to Division One two years later in 1990. Sadly, Eric was never given the opportunity to turn out for Sunderland in the top flight and during the 1990 close-season he was transferred to Carlisle United. After one season at Brunton Park he decided to retire from the game and pursue a career in the media before taking over a farm on the outskirts of Sunderland.

As well as being an outstanding performer on the pitch, Eric was a hugely popular figure with supporters during his time at Portman Road and in 2012 he was inducted into Ipswich Town's 'Hall of Fame'.

ERIC Gates

PLAYER PROFILE

DATE OF BIRTH:	28 June 1955
PLACE OF BIRTH:	Ferryhill, County Durham
IPSWICH TOWN:	384 Appearances · 96 Goals
1980/81 UEFA CUP:	11 Appearances · 1 Goal

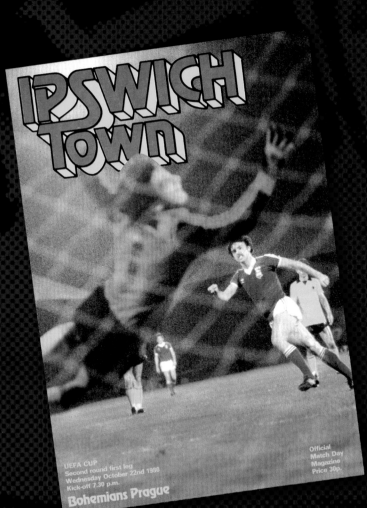

IPSWICH
TOWN

UEFA CUP
Second round first leg
Wednesday October 22nd 1980
Kick-off 7.30 p.m.
Bohemians Prague

Official
Match Day
Magazine
Price 30p.

IPSWICH TOWN 3

Wark (48, 55), Beattie (85)

BOHEMIANS 0

Wednesday 22 October 1980
Portman Road · Attendance: 17,163

IPSWICH TOWN:
PAUL COOPER · GEORGE BURLEY · STEVE McCALL · MICK MILLS
RUSSELL OSMAN · TERRY BUTCHER · JOHN WARK · ARNOLD MÜHREN
PAUL MARINER · ALAN BRAZIL · ERIC GATES
SUB USED: KEVIN BEATTIE

BOHEMIANS:
ZDENĚK HRUŠKA · KAREL ROUBÍČEK · ZDENĚK PROKEŠ
JIŘÍ ONDRA · FRANTIŠEK JAKUBEC · ANTONÍN PANENKA
JAROSLAV NĚMEC · ZDENĚK KOUKAL · PAVEL CHALOUPKA
PŘEMYSL BIČOVSKÝ · MILAN ČERMÁK · SUB USED: JIŘÍ KOTRBA

REFEREE: OLE AMUNDSEN (DENMARK)

**UEFA CUP WINNERS
1980/81
40TH ANNIVERSARY**

2nd
ROUND
FIRST LEG

Despite their defeat in Greece, Ipswich were going great guns in the domestic game and by the time the second round tie against Bohemians Prague came around they were sitting proudly at the top of Division One after 1-1 draws with both Liverpool and Manchester United. They had also progressed in the League Cup, claiming local 'bragging rights' with a terrific 3-1 victory over arch rivals Norwich City in the third-round replay at Carrow Road.

The Czech side represented a tough challenge for Robson's team having finished third in the table the previous season, and their team included a number of quality players including their star man Antonin Panenka. One of the most popular players in Czech football, Panenka had picked up 45 caps for his country and is perhaps best remembered for his audacious chip when he deceived German 'keeper Sepp Maier in the penalty shoot-out to clinch the 1976 European Championship for his country.

Bobby Robson was well aware of the ability of the Czech side...

"I've been to see them play and I like the Czechs - I think they are good footballers, tough and durable with good technique."

Ipswich were without Frans Thijssen who had pulled a hamstring against Manchester United four days earlier, an injury that would also rule the Dutch midfielder out of the reckoning for the return leg in Prague. Predictably perhaps, the Czech side set out to frustrate Ipswich from the kick-off and were soon proving difficult to break down.

The home side were enjoying the lion's share of possession in the opening half, but clear opportunities were few and far between with both Mariner and Brazil having the best opportunities only to be denied by the Bohemians 'keeper. Little was seen of the visitors as an attacking force with star man Panenka largely anonymous and as the first half drew to a close, it appeared that Robson's team were facing a tough challenge to gain any sort of advantage in the home leg.

However, the half-time break was to prove decisive with Robson changing his tactics and encouraging his team to up the pace and be more attack-minded.

John Wark had been Town's hero in the first round tie against Aris Salonika at Portman Road when he netted four goals, and again he was the man who broke the deadlock just three minutes after the restart. The move began out on the right with Mills who picked out Gates on the corner of the box. Even though he was tightly marked, he was able to drop his shoulder and turn inside before laying the ball across the edge of the box for the oncoming Wark to rifle a terrific shot into the corner of the net low to the 'keeper's left.

The goal came as a huge relief to the Portman Road faithful and seven minutes later they were celebrating a second, and yet again it was Wark who delivered the telling finish.

This time the move started on the left with Mühren weaving his way through a couple of challenges before feeding a perfect ball through for Brazil whose left-foot shot struck the foot of the post only for Wark to race in and slot the ball into the net.

Robson's team were now very much in command although there was still the danger of the visitors snatching a vital away goal on the break.

As the game moved into the final minutes Bobby Robson made a tactical change bringing on Kevin Beattie for the injured John Wark. It was a massive moment for Beattie who had played very little football in the two previous seasons due to a problematic knee injury and he could not have marked his return to fitness in a more dramatic fashion.

awarded a free-kick twenty yards from goal after Gates' surging run was halted with a blatant body-check and when Mills rolled the ball to his left, Beattie strode up to send a stunning left-foot rising drive high into the net via the underside of the bar.

The goal, which would be so important in the final analysis, almost lifted the roof at Portman Road and turned the tie firmly in the favour of Bobby Robson's Blues.

A true legend at Portman Road, Kevin Beattie was held in such high esteem by Ipswich Town supporters that in three separate polls they voted him the club's greatest ever player.

Born in Carlisle, Kevin was one of nine siblings and first came to prominence with local youth team Blackfriars. So impressive were his performances in local football, Kevin was invited to Liverpool for trials, but when no one turned up at Lime Street Station to meet him, he promptly headed home assuming they were no longer interested. Liverpool manager Bill Shankly later admitted that missing out on Kevin Beattie was probably the biggest mistake he ever made in managerial career.

There's no question that Liverpool's loss was very much Ipswich Town's gain and after only three years at Portman Road Kevin was making his first-team debut against Manchester United at Old Trafford on the opening day of the 1972/73 season. Playing in the centre of Town's defence alongside seasoned campaigner Allan Hunter, Kevin was an absolute revelation with his pace and power, quickly cementing his place in the side and he went on to make an incredible 49 league and cup appearances in his first season. The following season he was an ever-present in the side and was voted English football's 'Young Player of the Season', becoming the first player to lift the new award.

Predictably, international recognition quickly followed and after being capped by England at Under-23 level he stepped up to senior level when manager Don Revie selected him to play against Cyprus at Wembley in April 1975. England's 5-0 victory was notable for all the goals being scored by Malcolm MacDonald although Kevin was desperately unlucky not to mark his debut with a goal when he had an effort ruled out for a foul on the goalkeeper. Arguably his most memorable England performance came in the 5-1 demolition of Scotland in the 1974/75 Home International Championship when he netted his only goal for his country, a brilliant looping header.

In 1978, Kevin was a member of Town's FA Cup-winning side and in the 1980 close season he was one of a group of Ipswich players that headed out to Budapest to film 'Escape to Victory' during which he apparently beat Sylvester Stallone in an arm-wrestling contest, much to the annoyance of the Hollywood star. At this point the future certainly looked bright for Kevin, but just when a lengthy career beckoned, a series of injuries began to seriously jeopardise his progress at both club and country level.

During the 1980/81 season, his appearances for Ipswich were limited, although he did play in eight of the club's UEFA Cup games and few can forget his dramatic late goal against Bohemians when he came off the bench to rifle home a stunning free-kick to secure a 3-0 victory. Sadly, a broken arm sustained in the FA Cup semi-final against Manchester City denied him a place in the final, although few could have envisaged that this would also be his last game for the club. Persistent injuries had taken their toll and while he attempted comebacks with first Colchester and then Middlesbrough, he was forced to finish his career in non-league football. Away from football, Kevin co-wrote his autobiography 'The Beat' in 1998' and remained a popular figure in Ipswich, returning to the public eye with his matchday work on local radio from 2008 onwards. He died of a heart attack, aged 64 in September 2018.

Kevin Beattie will always hold a special place in the hearts of Ipswich Town supporters who voted him their 'Player of the Year' in 1972/73 and 1973/74 and he was inducted into Ipswich Town's 'Hall of Fame' in 2008. Perhaps the finest compliment came from Bobby Robson who described him quite simply as 'one of English football's all-time greats'.

KEVIN WITH CLIVE WOODS AFTER THE 1978 FA CUP SEMI-FINAL 3-0 WIN OVER WBA

ON ENGLAND DUTY

KEVIN Beattie

PLAYER PROFILE

DATE OF BIRTH:	18 December 1953
PLACE OF BIRTH:	Carlisle
IPSWICH TOWN:	307 Appearances · 32 Goals
1980/81 UEFA CUP:	8 Appearances · 1 Goal

BOHEMIANS 2

Mičinec (2), Panenka (52)

IPSWICH TOWN 0

Wednesday 5 November 1980
Stadion Ďolíček · Attendance: 15,000

BOHEMIANS:

JAN POŠTULKA · ZDENĚK PROKEŠ · JIŘÍ ONDRA
FRANTIŠEK JAKUBEC · ANTONÍN PANENKA · JAROSLAV NĚMEC
ZDENĚK KOUKAL · PAVEL CHALOUPKA · PŘEMYSL BIČOVSKÝ
TIBOR MIČINEC · MILAN ČERMÁK · SUB USED: JIŘÍ KOTRBA

IPSWICH TOWN:

LAURIE SIVELL · GEORGE BURLEY · TERRY BUTCHER · MICK MILLS
RUSSELL OSMAN · KEVIN BEATTIE · JOHN WARK · ARNOLD MÜHREN
ERIC GATES · ALAN BRAZIL · STEVE McCALL
SUB USED: ROBIN TURNER

REFEREE: PAOLO CASARIN (ITALY)

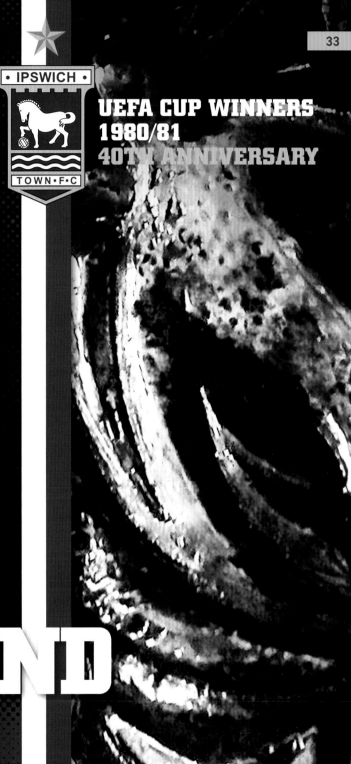

IPSWICH
TOWN·F·C

UEFA CUP WINNERS
1980/81
40TH ANNIVERSARY

2nd
ROUND
SECOND LEG

Town's interest in the League Cup had ended with a 2-1 defeat against Birmingham City at St. Andrews, but the players were still in great spirits when they headed out to Prague for the second leg, with singing on the flight and on the coach to the hotel, where they would spend most of the time due to the extreme cold. Confidence was high as the players arrived at the Stadion Doliček for the game even though the sub-zero temperatures forced them to wear extra layers of clothing, apart from Kevin Beattie who insisted on wearing his normal short-sleeved shirt.

Injuries to key players forced Ipswich to change their line-up with long-serving goalkeeper Lawrie Sivell coming in for Paul Cooper and Kevin Beattie getting a rare start replacing Paul Mariner. Little had been seen of Bohemians as an attacking force in the first leg at Portman Road, but on home soil, with temperatures down to minus four degrees at kick-off, they were soon proving to be a bit of a handful for the Ipswich defence.

With a three-goal lead from the first leg, the odds were stacked heavily in Ipswich Town's favour, but just as they had done in Greece in the previous round, their advantage was quickly eroded with an early goal from the home side. With only two minutes on the clock, the Town defenders were caught napping when they failed to clear a long ball into the box allowing Mičinec to nip in and slide the ball past Sivell to send the home fans wild with delight.

The home side now had the upper hand, but Ipswich were still able to provide a threat on the Bohemians' goal with Wark having three headers well saved by Poštulka.

Nevertheless, it was the home side that came nearest to scoring when Beattie made an acrobatic clearance off the line after a header from Chaloupka came down off the underside of the bar.

Bohemians were now putting Town under increasing pressure with only last-ditch defending keeping them at bay and when the half-time whistle blew, it was a relieved Ipswich team that headed to the dressing room.

Despite Town's two-goal advantage, Bohemians' dominance in the first half suggested that the tie was still finely balanced and on 52 minutes that balance swung firmly in favour of the home side when they grabbed a second goal. There seemed little danger when Sivell raced from his box to clear a long ball downfield only for the referee to penalise the Ipswich 'keeper for a foul on Mičinec just outside the box. Star man Panenka stepped up to take the kick and in typical fashion, he curled a wonderful right-foot shot over the defensive wall and into the corner of the net giving Sivell absolutely no chance. The goal prompted mass celebrations among the home fans who could now sense victory and with 36 minutes still remaining things were beginning to look bleak for the visitors.

At times during the remainder of the game, Ipswich came under intense pressure, but to a man they stood firm and defended brilliantly with Beattie in particular putting in an outstanding performance.

On 65 minutes Bobby Robson had brought on Robin Turner to replace Alan Brazil and ironically the striker almost grabbed an unlikely goal in the closing minutes when he met Beattie's left-wing cross only to see his goalbound effort strike a defender on the head and rebound to safety.

Moments later the final whistle blew to signal relieved celebrations among the Ipswich players and travelling fans. It had been another close-run thing and Town's resolve had been tested to the limit by a tough Czech side, but they had survived and had made it through to the next round, albeit by the narrowest of margins.

The following day, the press were unanimous in their praise of Kevin Beattie who had produced a 'Man of the Match' performance and appeared to be very much back to top form. Beattie later recalled the game against the Czech side and in particular the freezing temperatures,

"I always wear short sleeves for the simple reason that I prefer them. Anyway, as soon as the game started I forgot about the cold. I had other things on my mind. We had to take a lot of pressure, but I enjoyed the game. In the end I thought we got the better of the Czechs because there seemed to be a lot of frustration about their play as the game wore on."

George Burley holds the unique distinction of being the first Ipswich Town player to go on to manage the club. An outstanding full-back who gave the club great service during his playing career, George was spotted as a youngster playing local football in Ayrshire and joined Town as an apprentice in 1972.

His elevation to the first team the following season could hardly have been more daunting when he was given the job of marking George Best in an away fixture at Old Trafford. So impressive was his performance, George remained in the side for the remainder of the season with his forays into opposition territory soon leading to many Ipswich attacks. In 1977 Ipswich Town supporters voted him their 'Player of the Year' and twelve months later he picked up an FA Cup-winners medal following their memorable 1-0 victory over Arsenal at Wembley.

Having already been capped by Scotland at U21 and U23 level, George won his first full cap in 3-0 defeat at the hand of Wales in May 1979 and would eventually go on the represent his country eleven times.

He was a key member of Town's 1980/81 UEFA Cup squad and would surely have picked up a winners medal but, after playing in the first five games, his season came to a shuddering halt in an FA Cup third round tie at Shrewsbury when he sustained severe knee ligament damage. The injury was so bad that at one point there were doubts over George's future career prospects and only the skills of top surgeon David Dandy allowed him to make a full recovery.

His playing career at Portman Road, during which he had made 500 first-team appearances, lasted until September 1985 when he joined Sunderland in a £40,000 transfer, teaming up with Eric Gates who had joined the Roker Park club a few weeks earlier. George spent three seasons on Wearside before moving to Gillingham followed by a spell north of the border with first Motherwell and then Ayr United who gave him his first chance in management in 1991. Three years later, after a brief spell in charge at Gillingham, he made a sentimental return to Ipswich to take over as manager following the departure of John Lyall.

George spent eight years in charge at Ipswich, taking the club into the Premiership in 2000 via the play-offs and a fifth-place finish in his first season in the top flight brought European football back to Portman Road for the first time since 1982. His efforts earned him the Premier League Manager of the Season award, but his success was short lived and after Town were relegated the following season, his contract was terminated by mutual agreement.

George's career in football management continued with Derby County, Hearts and Southampton before he was invited to take over as manager of Scotland in January 2008. However, his spell in charge of the national team lasted less than two years following a string of disappointing results during which he won just three of the fourteen games he was in charge.

In 2009 George was inducted into Ipswich Town's 'Hall of Fame' before returning to football management with Crystal Palace and then Cypriot side Apollon Limassol although both appointments were short-lived.

GEORGE
Burley

PLAYER PROFILE

DATE OF BIRTH:	3 June 1956
PLACE OF BIRTH:	Cumnock, Scotland
IPSWICH TOWN:	500 Appearances · 11 Goals
1980/81 UEFA CUP:	5 Appearances

UEFA CUP
Third round first leg
Wednesday November 26th 1980
Kick-off 7.30 p.m.
RTS Widzew Łódź

Official
Match Day
Magazine
Price 30p.

IPSWICH TOWN 5

Wark (22, 44, 78), Brazil (41), Mariner (70)

WIDZEW ŁÓDŹ 0

Wednesday 26 November 1980
Portman Road · Attendance: 20,445

IPSWICH TOWN:

PAUL COOPER · MICK MILLS · STEVE McCALL · FRANS THIJSSEN
RUSSELL OSMAN · TERRY BUTCHER · JOHN WARK · ARNOLD MÜHREN
PAUL MARINER · ALAN BRAZIL · ERIC GATES
SUBS USED: KEVIN BEATTIE · KEVIN O'CALLAGHAN

WIDZEW ŁÓDŹ:

JÓZEF MŁYNARCZYK · WŁADYSŁAW ANTONI ŹMUDA
BOGUSŁAW PLICH · ANDRZEJ MOŻEJKO · ANDRZEJ GRĘBOSZ
MAREK PIĘTA · MIROSŁAW TŁOKIŃSKI · ZDZISŁAW ROZBORSKI
JAN JEŻEWSKI · WŁODZIMIERZ SMOLAREK · ZBIGNIEW BONIEK
SUB USED: PIOTR ROMKE

REFEREE: ROBERT WURTZ (FRANCE)

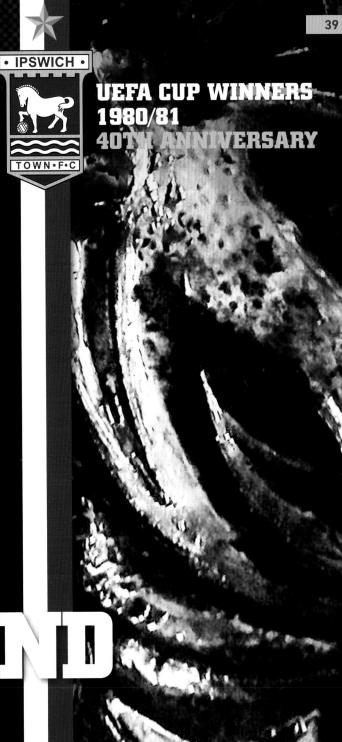

UEFA CUP WINNERS
1980/81
40TH ANNIVERSARY

3rd
ROUND
FIRST LEG

Another Wark hat-trick helps Blues blitz Widzew Łódź

The draw for round three once again gave Ipswich home advantage in the first leg and also another trip behind the Iron Curtain, this time to Poland when they were paired with Widzew Łódź. The Polish side had finished as runners-up in their domestic league in the previous three seasons and were again occupying second spot.

Their team included a number of outstanding players, the most famous was their skipper Zbigniew Boniek, a man with almost fifty caps for his country and widely regarded as one of the greatest players in the history of Polish football. Ipswich were also occupying second place in the English First Division, losing top spot to Aston Villa after their first league defeat of the season, a 1-0 reverse at Brighton.

Having knocked Juventus and Manchester United out of the competition in the previous rounds, Widzew Łódź were clearly going to provide a tough challenge for Bobby Robson's team. Making sure he did his homework, the Ipswich manager had received a full report on the strengths and weaknesses of the Polish side from United manager Dave Sexton as well as sending Bobby Ferguson, his number two, out to Poland to watch Widzew's away victory over Zagłębie Sosnowiec.

Immediately prior to the match, Bobby Robson was somewhat taken aback when the Widzew Łódź coach pulled him to one side and made him an unusual proposition. The Ipswich boss later recalled...

"I think they underestimated us and I remember a stupid conversation with their coach before the game who actually wanted to bet me with money on the result. It was the first time ever in my life that a coach from the opposition had actually wanted to have a money bet on the result, I just couldn't believe it!"

The Polish team's coach was obviously confident, probably due to the fact that his side had dumped Manchester United out of the competition, but by the end of the game, he will no doubt have been relieved that Bobby Robson didn't accept the wager as a rampant Ipswich side raced to an emphatic 5-0 first-leg victory.

The opening goal came on 22 minutes when Gates won the ball in midfield to release Mühren down the left and when the Dutchman crossed, the ball was headed on to Brazil out on the right. Even though he was tightly marked the Scot turned outside to send in a low cross which was only half cleared allowing Thijssen to win possession and lay the ball off to Wark who fired home from close range.

Moments later it was almost two when Brazil picked up a loose clearance on the right and when he laid the ball to Mühren 25 yards from goal, the Dutchman unleashed a terrific left-foot drive which beat the 'keeper all ends up, but smashed against the foot of the post and rebounded to safety.

At this stage Ipswich were laying siege on the visitor's goal and it came as no surprise when they doubled their advantage, although this time it was an absolute gift after a terrible error by Młynarczyk. There was no danger when the Polish 'keeper dropped his attempted clearance short, allowing Thijssen to dispossess the defender and lay the ball through to Brazil who steered a left-foot drive high into the net.

Amazingly, three minutes later, the third goal arrived following a brilliant flowing move involving Thijssen, Gates and then Mühren who released McCall down the left. The full-back swung in a delightful cross to pick out Mariner at the far post and when his goalbound effort was blocked, Wark followed up in typical fashion to ram the ball home from close range.

The Polish side looked shell-shocked as they trooped off to the dressing room at half-time, but there was to be little respite during the second period as Ipswich continued to dominate the game, playing the sort of brilliant attacking football that had now become their trademark in the English game.

On 70 minutes the fourth goal duly arrived, and what a beauty it was. Mühren was the architect out on the right, delivering a delightful cross with the outside of his left foot to pick out Mariner racing into the box to rocket the ball into the roof of the net with a brilliant diving header.

With 20 minutes remaining Robson brought on Kevin O'Callaghan to replace Alan Brazil and the 20-year-old winger was soon in the thick of the action setting up the final goal of the night. Wark won the ball inside his own half to release O'Callaghan out on the left.

The winger left the full-back in his wake as he raced down the wing to send in a cross which was headed goalwards by Mariner and as the 'keeper advanced, Wark nipped in to volley home and complete his hat-trick.

It had been a superb performance by the Ipswich team and a highly satisfying result for their manager, particularly considering the pre-match antics of his opposite number. The only disappointment of an otherwise brilliant night was an ankle injury to Mick Mills which required ten stitches and would put the Ipswich skipper out action for some weeks.

At the end of the game a beaming Bobby Robson said...

"There were spells in the first half when I've never seen us play better. It was a super display; we destroyed them and ran them ragged."

Initially a youth player with Celtic, Alan Brazil was spotted by Bobby Robson's scouting network in 1977 and was soon persuaded to move south of the border to join Ipswich Town. Alan quickly developed an eye for goal in youth team football, eventually prompting Bobby Robson to hand him his first-team debut when he came off the bench against Manchester United at Portman Road in January 1978.

However, it was the following season when he really began to establish himself as a first-team regular and after scoring his first goal for the club in a 1-1 draw with Nottingham Forest, he went on to make 19 appearances, netting five goals in a campaign that saw Town finish in 6th place in Division One.

Capped by Scotland at Youth and Under-21 level, Alan soon became a key player in the Ipswich attack, teaming up alongside Paul Mariner to form a potent strike force that helped Ipswich mount a serious challenge for the League title. His strong running style and his ability to hold the ball and turn opponents soon made him a great favourite with the Portman Road faithful and it came as no surprise when he received international recognition with his first full international cap for Scotland against Poland in May 1980. Alan went on to win 13 caps for his country and was a member of the Scotland squad that appeared in the 1982 World Cup Finals in Spain.

Brazil played in every game of Ipswich Town's 1980/81 UEFA Cup-winning triumph and the following season he finished second top scorer in Division One with 22 goals, including a truly memorable performance at Portman Road when he netted all of Town's goals in a 5-2 triumph over second in the table Southampton.

In all, Alan scored 80 goals for Ipswich during his six years at Portman Road before severing his ties with the club in March 1983 to join Tottenham Hotspur in a £425,000 transfer. A year later he joined Manchester United in another big money move but with a recurring back injury soon proving to be problematic, his time at Old Trafford became something of a disappointment and in January 1986 he was transferred to Coventry City.

There followed a short-lived move to Queens Park Rangers and then spells playing in Australia and Switzerland before he returned to England to finish his career in non-league football. Alan hung up his boots at the end of the 1989/90 season and initially ran The Black Adder pub in Ipswich before moving into media work, eventually carving out a highly successful career with Talk Sport.

ALAN Brazil

PLAYER PROFILE

DATE OF BIRTH:	15 June 1959
PLACE OF BIRTH:	Govan, Glasgow
IPSWICH TOWN:	210 Appearances · 80 Goals
1980/81 UEFA CUP:	12 Appearances · 1 Goal

WIDZEW ŁÓDŹ 1
Pięta (55)

IPSWICH TOWN 0

Wednesday 10 December 1980
Stadion Widzewa · Attendance: 9,000

WIDZEW ŁÓDŹ:

JERZY KLEPCZYŃSKI · KRZYSZTOF SURLIT · BOGUSŁAW PLICH
ANDRZEJ MOŻEJKO · ANDRZEJ GRĘBOSZ · MIROSŁAW TŁOKIŃSKI
PIOTR ROMKE · MAREK PIĘTA · JAN JEŻEWSKI
ZDZISŁAW ROZBORSKI · WŁODZIMIERZ SMOLAREK
SUB USED: JANUSZ LISIAK

IPSWICH TOWN:

PAUL COOPER · GEORGE BURLEY · STEVE McCALL · FRANS THIJSSEN
RUSSELL OSMAN · TERRY BUTCHER · JOHN WARK · ARNOLD MÜHREN
PAUL MARINER · ALAN BRAZIL · ERIC GATES
SUBS USED: KEVIN BEATTIE · KEVIN O'CALLAGHAN

REFEREE: JAN REDELFS (WEST GERMANY)

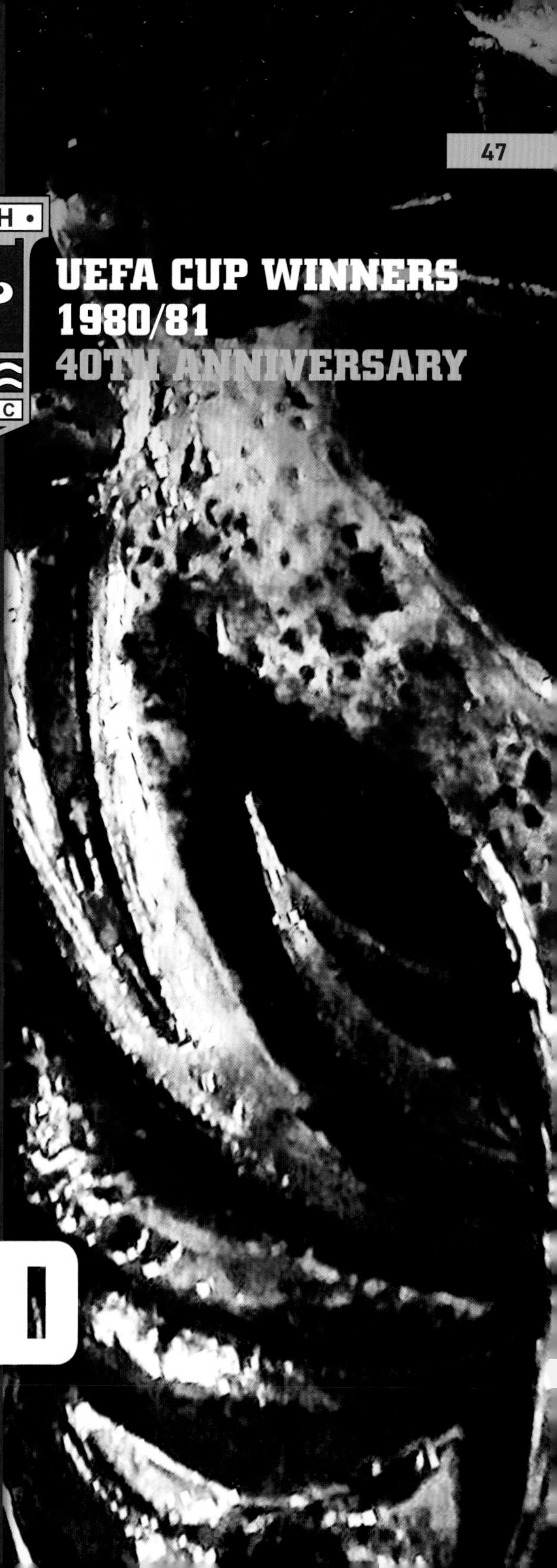

IPSWICH
TOWN·F·C

UEFA CUP WINNERS
1980/81
40TH ANNIVERSARY

3rd
ROUND
SECOND LEG

PAUL MARINER

If conditions had been particularly cold in Ipswich's previous away leg in Prague, they were nothing compared to the arctic conditions they encountered in Poland for the second leg against Widzew Łódź. When the Ipswich party arrived in the Polish mining town, temperatures had dipped to minus fourteen degrees and with the pitch covered in snow and ice, there seemed little chance of the game going ahead.

Amazingly, the referee thought that the pitch was fine, although the UEFA official representative had told Bobby Robson that in his opinion, the pitch was unplayable and he would be quite happy if the Ipswich boss asked for the game to be postponed. However, he also added that if the game did not go ahead, it could not be re-scheduled until March due to the severe winter weather conditions that were imminent. Faced with his team's gruelling domestic programme and given that they held a five-goal advantage from the first leg, Robson somewhat reluctantly agreed to the game going ahead.

Apart from the arctic temperatures. the Ipswich players were also to experience a country still suffering the effects of the Cold War, as John Wark recalls...

"The thing I'll always remember from Poland were the queues for the chocolate ration in the freezing cold, in some cases stretching up to 200 yards. It was hard to imagine that here we were, almost into the 1980s, yet this sort of thing was still going on. I recall some of the lads took pity on the youngsters that gathered outside of our hotel and gave them bars of chocolate, even signing the wrappers for them!"

Ipswich were forced to leave out skipper Mick Mills who had sustained a gashed ankle in the first leg at Portman Road. Predictably, the game itself soon turned into a farcical affair with players from both sides struggling to keep their feet, let alone produce any kind of flowing football, the orange pitch markings in the snow simply adding to the sense of occasion. The home side were missing their star player Zbigniew Boniek, but its doubtful whether even he could have made any sort of impact on a surface that looked more like a skating rink than the stage of a top European game.

Once again, Kevin Beattie defied the severe weather wearing only a short-sleeved shirt and shorts whereas the rest of his colleagues piled on various layers of clothing. The first half had passed without any serious attempt on goal, but ten minutes after the break, the Poles broke the deadlock. A mix up in the middle of the park saw Ipswich lose possession and when the ball was played into the box, Pięta was able to avoid the challenges of the Town defenders to slot the ball home. The goal gave the home fans some hope, many no doubt thinking of how Ipswich had almost thrown away a four-goal lead in the first round, but their team were unable to breach the visitors' rearguard again. There were plenty of hopeful balls into the box and a couple of half-chances, but Cooper dealt with everything that came his way with ease as the Ipswich rearguard held firm to ensure their team progressed into the next round.

It was a particularly good night for Terry Butcher who was superb in the heart of the Ipswich defence, and also celebrated his 100th first-team appearance for the club.

Now comfortably into the quarter-finals, Bobby Robson and his team's quest for European glory was now put on hold until March, allowing them to concentrate on domestic challenges at home. In all, they played 13 league and five FA Cup games during this period, losing only once in a thrilling 5-3 league defeat at the hands of Tottenham Hotspur, and by the time they returned to European action they were still sitting top of Division One and had also progressed into the quarter-finals of the FA Cup. In round three they had knocked out title-rivals Aston Villa with Paul Mariner netting the only goal of the game at Portman Road. Then came victories over Shrewsbury Town and Charlton Athletic, although the Shrewsbury win had come at a price after George Burley sustained an injury that would keep him out for the rest of the season.

The games were now beginning to come thick and fast and if their dreams of a remarkable treble were to stay alive, Ipswich now had to overcome perhaps the toughest challenge of all, when the UEFA Cup quarter-final draw paired them with St-Étienne of France, one of Europe's finest teams that boasted a galaxy of top international stars in their ranks.

In many ways Steve McCall was one of the unsung heroes of Ipswich Town's 1980/81 UEFA Cup-winning team. He rarely grabbed the headlines, yet his consistent performances on the left side of Town's defence were a key factor in the team's success. A versatile player who was equally at home in defence or midfield, Steve was born in Carlisle and was a product of Town's youth policy, winning youth international honours for England at a time when Brian Clough was in charge.

He made his first-team debut in a UEFA cup-tie against Skeid Oslo in September 1979, although it was the following campaign when he really became established as a first-team regular, making 48 appearances in a season that stretched to 66 games. England B honours followed and at his peak he could count himself desperately unlucky not to have been capped by his country at full international level.

After the UEFA Cup success Steve was virtually an ever-present in the Ipswich first team missing only one FA Cup game in three seasons. In all, he made well over 300 appearances for Ipswich Town and his outstanding career at Portman Road was rightly recognised in 2017 when he was inducted into the club's Hall of Fame.

In June 1987, after almost nine years at Portman Road, Steve joined Sheffield Wednesday in a £400,000 transfer. However, he was unable to replicate the level of success he had enjoyed at Ipswich with his progress at Hillsborough blighted by a series of injuries. Nevertheless, he made five appearances in the club's 1990/91 League Cup run although he wasn't selected for the final at Wembley where they recorded a memorable 1-0 victory over Manchester United.

Steve spent four seasons with Wednesday before joining Plymouth Argyle where he enjoyed a brief spell as caretaker-manager in 1995 before being replaced by Neil Warnock. He then spent two seasons with Torquay United where he fulfilled a life-time ambition by playing at Wembley in the 1998 Third Division Play-Off final against Colchester United, although the game ended in disappointment with a 1-0 defeat.

Steve then returned to Plymouth where he spent two years before hanging up his boots at the end of the 1999/2000 season. Soon afterwards, he joined former teammate George Burley back at Ipswich where he was appointed European scouting co-ordinator, before eventually progressing through the ranks to first-team coach.

STEVE McCall

PLAYER PROFILE

DATE OF BIRTH:	15 October 1960
PLACE OF BIRTH:	Carlisle
IPSWICH TOWN:	329 Appearances · 12 Goals
1980/81 UEFA CUP:	10 Appearances

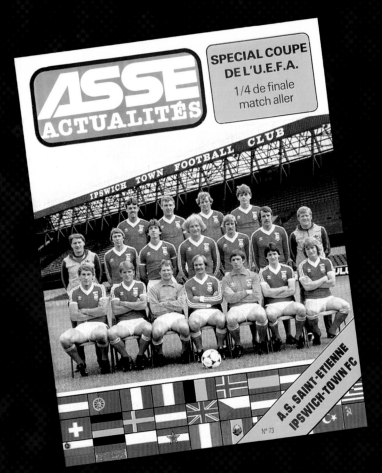

ST-ÉTIENNE 1
Rep (16)

IPSWICH TOWN 4
Mariner (28, 57), Mühren (47), Wark (76)

Wednesday 4 March 1981
Stade Geoffroy-Guichard, St-Étienne
Attendance: 42,000

ST-ÉTIENNE:

JEAN CASTANEDA · PATRICK BATTISTON · JEAN-LOUIS ZANON
BERNARD GARDON · CHRISTIAN LOPEZ · GÉRARD JANVION
JOHNNY REP · JEAN-FRANÇOIS LARIOS · LAURENT ROUSSEY
MICHEL PLATINI · LAURENT PAGANELLI
SUB USED: JACQUES ZIMAKO.

IPSWICH TOWN:

PAUL COOPER · MICK MILLS · TERRY BUTCHER · FRANS THIJSSEN
RUSSELL OSMAN · KEVIN BEATTIE · JOHN WARK · ARNOLD MÜHREN
PAUL MARINER · ALAN BRAZIL · ERIC GATES

REFEREE: NICOLAE RAINEA (ROMANIA)

IPSWICH TOWN·F·C

**UEFA CUP WINNERS
1980/81
40TH ANNIVERSARY**

THE
quarter
FINAL
FIRST LEG

Ipswich Town returned to European action in brilliant form having recorded no fewer than seven consecutive league and cup victories. Sitting in the stands for one of those games, a 3-1 home victory over Wolverhampton Wanderers, was St-Étienne manager Robert Herbin who promptly announced after the match.

"We have no chance, but we will do our best."

Bearing in mind that his team were regarded by many as favourites for the tie and boasted the likes of Michel Platini, Johnny Rep and Christian Lopez in their ranks, this was seen as little more than an unconvincing attempt at pre-match psychology. Ironically however, the French manager could hardly have imagined how prophetic those words would be as his side were swept aside by a rampant Ipswich side that arguably, produced their greatest ever performance in European football.

The tie attracted massive interest among St-Étienne supporters and even though the all-ticket game was a sell-out, they started queuing more than five hours before kick-off, and by the time the two teams walked out onto the pitch, the noise inside the stadium was deafening.

Ipswich started strongly and should have taken the lead after ten minutes when after great work out on the right, Mariner picked out Gates inside the box in a great position, but his shot from ten yards flew over the bar. The visitors were made to rue that miss when, with 16 minutes on the clock, the stadium erupted when Dutch international Johnny Rep gave St-Étienne the lead. The goal came from a short corner out on the left and when the ball was whipped into the box Rep rose above the Ipswich defence to send a brilliant bullet header flying past Paul Cooper.

It was the worst possible start for Ipswich but undeterred, they soon regained their composure and on 28 minutes they grabbed an equaliser through Paul Mariner. The goal was engineered by Arnold Mühren who played a one-two with Gates before curling in a delightful cross to the far post which was met by Mariner who planted a towering header into the far corner of the net.

Mariner
opens the scoring...

...AND BUTCHER & WARK CELEBRATE

3-1
Paul Mariner pounces and puts the Blues in control

WARK CLIMBS MAJESTICALLY TO HEAD THE FOURTH

Soon afterwards St-Étienne broke out of defence to send Rep clear for the Dutchman to drive a right-foot shot past Cooper and into the net only for the effort to be ruled out for offside. They were close again a few minutes later when Rep sent in a shot from outside the box which was blocked by Cooper and when the ball dropped invitingly for Platini, the French international drove the ball narrowly wide of the far post.

The first half had been a fairly even affair with the home side perhaps creating the better of the chances, but few could have predicted the events of the second period as the home side were simply taken apart by a rampant Ipswich side that produced a truly brilliant display of fast, attacking football - this was Bobby Robson's side at their very best. Just two minutes after the break they were in front with a stunning goal from Mühren. The move began down the right flank with Mariner crossing the ball into box and when the St-Étienne defence failed to clear their lines, John Wark laid the ball back to Mühren who unleashed a stunning left-foot drive high into the corner of the net.

The stadium which had been bouncing at the start suddenly grew much quieter and ten minutes later it was stunned into complete silence when Ipswich netted a third goal. Again the move started down the right, this time with Brazil swinging in a left-foot cross which was met by Butcher beyond the far post and when his left-foot drive was parried by Jean Castaneda, Mariner stepped into to ram the loose ball into the net.

Ipswich were now in total control and it came as no surprise when, with fifteen minutes remaining, they added number four when Butcher broke down the left to cross for Wark to rise above the St-Étienne defence and send a brilliant looping header into the corner of the net. It had been a fantastic performance by Bobby Robson's team, and a result that he later reckoned would send 'shock waves' through European football. They may have endured a hostile reception from opposition supporters in the earlier rounds, but on this occasion the sporting St-Étienne fans were quick to applaud the Town players as they left the field of play.

Robert Herbin, the St-Étienne manager, was also quick to praise Bobby Robson's team referring to them as 'The English Steamroller!' Herbin added...

"We were outclassed by a better team on the day and we have a lot of lessons to learn. Basically, what happened was what I feared would happen. Ipswich are a complete team, young and dynamic. They have eleven good players and tonight Osman and Mariner were fantastic."

The delighted Ipswich players celebrated a momentous victory in typical style, although Mick Mills was slightly more subdued than his colleagues. The Town skipper explained,

"I feel it's very important that we keep our feet on the ground. I would love to be excited like everybody else, but I know what sort of programme we have coming up and if I can give a lead anywhere then I want to give a lead there. Obviously everybody will read the newspapers tomorrow morning and quite rightly enjoy the moment, but come Friday they will all be talking about Saturday's game against Nottingham Forest."

FRANS THIJSSEN, ARNOLD MÜHREN
AND PAUL MARINER TAKE IN THEIR EPIC VICTORY

Born in Bolton, Paul Mariner began his playing career as a part-timer with non-league Chorley whilst working in a tin can factory and was signed by Plymouth Argyle in 1973. A powerfully built centre-forward in the traditional mould, Paul's goalscoring exploits with the south-coast club quickly had first division scouts circling over Home Park and in 1976 Bobby Robson clinched his signature in a deal valued at £240,000 with Ipswich players Terry Austin and John Peddelty moving in the opposite direction.

Paul was immediately drafted into Town's first-team squad and made his debut in a 1-0 victory over Manchester United in front of a crowd of over 57,000 at Old Trafford. Thereafter, he was pretty much a regular in the side and finished the campaign with 13 league and cup goals to his credit.

So impressive was his impact in the top flight that just six months after signing for Town, Paul won his first international cap for his country, coming off the bench in England's 5-0 victory over Luxemburg at Wembley. He went on to win 35 caps for his country netting 13 goals and was an ever-present in the England team that played in the 1982 World Cup finals in Spain.

Paul also played in every game in Ipswich Town's glorious 1978 FA Cup campaign and he finished the season as the club's top scorer with 22 goals in all competitions. The season also marked the arrival on the first team scene of young Scottish striker Alan Brazil and the pair quickly formed a devastating strike partnership that would become the scourge of First Division defences in the years ahead.

In 1983, Paul picked up Town's Player of the Year award, so it came as a major surprise when, in February 1984, the club decided to sell their prize asset to Arsenal for £150,000. Paul spent two seasons at Highbury and then joined Portsmouth before finishing his playing career with first Wollongong City in Australia and then in the American Soccer League with Albany Capitals and San Francisco Bay. After ending his playing career he moved into coaching and management including a spell in charge at his first league club Plymouth Argyle in 2009/10.

Regarded by many as rivalling the legendary Ray Crawford as the finest centre-forward in the club's history, Paul was inducted into Ipswich Town's 'Hall of Fame' in 2011.

PAUL AT PLYMOUTH ARGYLE

...AND WITH ENGLAND

PAUL
Mariner

PLAYER PROFILE

DATE OF BIRTH:	22 May 1953
PLACE OF BIRTH:	Bolton, Lancashire
IPSWICH TOWN:	339 Appearances · 135 Goals
1980/81 UEFA CUP:	11 Appearances · 6 Goals

UEFA CUP
Quarter-final second leg
Wednesday March 18th 1981
Kick-off 7.30 p.m.

A.S. Saint Etienne

IPSWICH TOWN 3

Butcher (46), Wark (82 Pen), Mariner (89)

ST-ÉTIENNE 1

Zimako (80)

Wednesday 18 March 1981
Portman Road · Attendance: 30,141

IPSWICH TOWN:
PAUL COOPER · KEVIN STEGGLES · STEVE McCALL
FRANS THIJSSEN · RUSSELL OSMAN · TERRY BUTCHER
JOHN WARK · ARNOLD MÜHREN · PAUL MARINER · ALAN BRAZIL
ERIC GATES · SUBS USED: KEVIN O'CALLAGHAN · MICH D'AVRAY

ST-ÉTIENNE:
JEAN CASTANEDA · CHRISTIAN LOPEZ · GÉRARD JANVION
BERNARD GARDON · PATRICK BATTISTON · JEAN-LOUIS ZANON
MICHEL PLATINI · JEAN-FRANÇOIS LARIOS · JACQUES ZIMAKO
LAURENT ROUSSEY · JOHNNY REP

REFEREE: ERICH LINEMAYR (AUSTRIA)

**UEFA CUP WINNERS
1980/81
40TH ANNIVERSARY**

THE quarter FINAL
SECOND LEG

Ipswich faced three tough games before the return leg against St-Étienne beginning with a FA Cup quarter-final tie at Brian Clough's Nottingham Forest just three days after their UEFA Cup victory in France. The match at the City Ground turned out to be a real classic with Town leading 2-0, but eventually needing a late Frans Thijssen equaliser to earn a 3-3 draw. In the replay at Portman Road a single Arnold Mühren goal, a stunning volley from the edge of the box, settled the issue and earned Ipswich a place in the semi-finals to keep their treble hopes on course.

Then a resounding 3-0 home win over Tottenham Hotspur kept Town on top of the league, but the victory came with a price as Mick Mills was forced to leave the field with a dislocated shoulder following one of many dubious challenges by the Spurs players. After the game, with a number of his players nursing bumps and bruises, an angry Bobby Robson pulled no punches in his condemnation of the tactics employed by the North-London side.

With Mick Mills likely to be missing for a number of weeks and George Burley ruled out for the rest of the season, Ipswich were now missing their two regular full-backs for what was going to be a busy and critical part of the campaign. There was however, a major boost for the club when Town players literally swept the board in the two major national Player of the Year awards. John Wark picked up the PFA Player of the Year award with teammates Frans Thijssen and Arnold Mühren finishing second and third while the football writers opted for Thijssen as Footballer of the Year with Mick Mills as runner-up and Wark third. It was the first time ever that players from the same club had filled both the top three places.

Despite their heavy first-leg defeat, St-Étienne brought a strong contingent of travelling fans to Portman Road ,many of whom will no doubt have been eating large quantities of hamburgers in an effort to win a free return trip to Ipswich courtesy of a competition being run by their local McDonald's.

Given Town's habit of surrendering first-leg leads in the earlier rounds, Bobby Robson was adamant there would be no room for complacency...

"While our 4-1 lead from the first leg provides us with something of a cushion this evening, we are not being fooled into thinking that we simply have to go through the motions. Our opponents have no alternative but to attack and it will be our intention to score goals and put the match well beyond their reach."

PAUL MARINER LEADS OUT THE BLUES

The injuries to Mick Mills and George Burley meant that Bobby Robson was forced to reorganise his defence and he took the brave decision of giving 19-year-old right-back Kevin Steggles his first-team debut.

This must have been a daunting prospect for the youngster particularly when he was up against Dutch international Johnny Rep, a player regarded by many as the finest left-winger in European football. Nevertheless, the Ipswich full-back acquitted himself brilliantly in a defence that never looked like surrendering their first-leg advantage. Right from the kick-off, Town were in control and just as they had in the first leg, St-Étienne were struggling to contain the home side's dominance in the air and only a string of superb saves by French goalkeeper Jean Castaneda kept the home side at bay. However, one minute into the second period the French rearguard was finally breached after Ipswich won a free-kick out on the right.

Thijssen took the kick and his floated cross picked out Butcher storming into the box to send a great header into the corner of the net giving Castaneda no chance. Thereafter Town were cruising, but with ten minutes remaining, St-Étienne managed to pull a goal back when, after an excellent flowing move, Rep managed to break free of Steggles on the left for the first time in the game and crossed for Zimako to head home from close range.

Any hopes of a remarkable fight-back were soon extinguished however, when two minutes later, Ipswich regained the lead from the penalty spot when Larios handled in the box following a right-wing corner. The ever-clinical John Wark stepped up to take the kick and sent the 'keeper the wrong way to restore the home side's advantage. Then, in the last minute, Mariner put the final nail in the French side's coffin and again the goal came as a result of a set-play. This time the Blues won a free-kick 20 yards out to the right of goal and when Thijssen's right-foot kick found its way to Butcher, the central-defender sent in a terrific right-foot drive which Casteneda could only parry allowing Mariner to step in and sweep the ball into the net.

At the end of the match, the Ipswich players were rightly elated, none more so than young Kevin Steggles who had produced an outstanding display to nullify the threat of Johnny Rep...

"It was a big game for the club and I was determined not the let anyone down," he said. "I just concentrated on doing the simple things and didn't try anything too clever. I must say, I received terrific encouragement from all the other lads, especially Paul Cooper and Russell Osman. Johnny Rep is still a world class player and it was only in the last ten minutes or so that he got away from me. I don't want it to sound like an excuse, but I was really tired by then."

Over the two legs it had been a truly remarkable performance by Bobby Robson's team and the Ipswich manager later reflected on what he regarded as probably their greatest performance in Europe,

KEVIN STEGGLES

"It was without doubt one of the best, if not the best, performance by an English team in Europe. We had beaten a top European side 7-2 on aggregate over two legs in the last eight of a major tournament. Now that's some score and you have to have a really dishy team to achieve that sort of result - that's a measure of how good we actually were."

TERRY BUTCHER'S BULLET HEADER AND CELEBRATION

ALAN BRAZIL, ARNOLD MÜHREN, JOHN WARK AND FRANS THIJSSEN

MICHEL PLATINI & ARNOLD MÜHREN

John Wark also regards the first-leg victory over St-Étienne as their finest performance in the whole tournament, although he now reveals that a few of the players, himself included, went into the game with their ears still ringing following a severe dressing down from Bobby Robson on the eve of the game...

"On the Tuesday morning we did some light training, then the boss said we could go into town to relax and do some shopping. Unfortunately, a few of the lads considered the local bars infinitely more attractive than wandering around shops and we ended up having a few drinks, nothing excessive, just four or five pints. When we headed back to our hotel for our evening meal, Bobby Robson quickly sussed what had been going on and gave us the biggest bollocking you can imagine before announcing: 'You are all fined a week's wages!'

Now, for today's Premier League stars losing a week's wages is neither here or there, but in our day, we earned nothing like the players in the modern game. Sure, we were on reasonable money, but certainly couldn't afford to lose a week's wages and even leading up to the game, I couldn't help but wonder how I was going to explain to my wife why my next pay packet was light.

It didn't affect our performance though and even after conceding an early goal, on the night we were just brilliant and swept aside what many regarded as the finest side in European football. Back in the dressing room Bobby Robson was so elated, I don't think I've ever seen him so happy and he congratulated ever player individually before announcing: 'Oh, and by the way, those fines are cancelled!' What a relief!"

A giant of a man in every sense of the word, Terry Butcher was a rock in the heart of Ipswich Town's defence throughout the late 1970s and early '80s. Hard as nails and as brave as a lion, he would often risk personal injury when fighting for the cause and whenever his name is mentioned, it immediately conjures up an image of a battled-scarred hero with his head wrapped in blood-soaked bandages.

Born in Singapore where his father was stationed with the Royal Navy, Terry quickly showed an interest in the game when the family returned home to Suffolk, soon becoming a staunch Ipswich Town supporter. At school, the powerfully-built youngster began to excel at the game and was quickly attracting interest from a number of top clubs including Town's arch-rivals Norwich City who invited him to Carrow Road for trials. However, as soon as Ipswich threw their hat into the ring, there was only one club Terry was going to join.

He signed apprentice forms at Portman Road in August 1976 and soon progressed through the ranks before making his first-team debut in an away fixture at Everton towards the end of the 1977/78 season. Whilst his elevation to the first eleven came just too soon to secure an appearance in Town's 1978 FA Cup triumph, Terry soon became a regular, teaming up alongside Allan Hunter before eventually forming a formidable central-defensive partnership with Russell Osman.

After picking up seven England U21 caps, he made his first full international appearance for his country when he was selected to play in a friendly international against Australia in May 1980. Terry went on to give sterling service to his country, winning 77 caps in an England career that saw him play in three World Cup finals and also enjoy the honour of captaining the side.

His swashbuckling performances were always the trademark of his game and few can forget his heroic display against Sweden in 1989 when he sustained a serious head injury, yet carried on bravely to the end, finishing the game literally covered in blood.

As bad as this injury was, it was nothing compared to the horrific incident in an FA Cup game at Luton some years earlier when Terry was accidentally kicked in the face by Brian Stein that left him literally fighting for his life due to the massive loss of blood. Only an emergency blood transfusion and intricate surgery saved his life and it was some months before he was able to return to first-team action.

Terry played in every game in Town's 1980/81 UEFA Cup success and his headed goal against Cologne in the semi-final second leg was possibly the most satisfying moment of his entire Ipswich career as it secured their place in the final. His truly brilliant first-team career at Ipswich spanned eight years and when Mick Mills left the club in 1982, Terry was appointed club captain, a position he held until 1986 when he was sold to Rangers. He was voted Town's Player of the Year in 1985 and 1986 and was inducted into Ipswich Town's 'Hall of Fame' in 2010. Terry continued his playing career with Coventry City and Sunderland and also managed both clubs before a short spell with Clydebank brought his career in the game to a close.

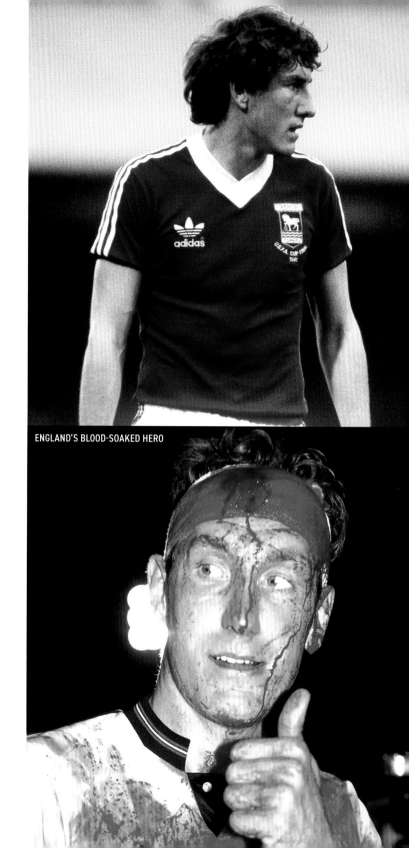

ENGLAND'S BLOOD-SOAKED HERO

71

TERRY
Butcher

PLAYER PROFILE

DATE OF BIRTH:	28 December 1958
PLACE OF BIRTH:	Singapore
IPSWICH TOWN:	351 Appearances · 21 Goals
1980/81 UEFA CUP:	12 Appearances · 2 Goals

IPSWICH TOWN 1

Wark (38)

FC COLOGNE 0

Wednesday 8 April 1981
Portman Road · Attendance: 24,780

IPSWICH TOWN:
PAUL COOPER · MICK MILLS · STEVE McCALL · FRANS THIJSSEN
RUSSELL OSMAN · TERRY BUTCHER · JOHN WARK · ARNOLD MÜHREN
PAUL MARINER · ALAN BRAZIL · ERIC GATES · SUBS USED: KEVIN
BEATTIE · KEVIN O'CALLAGHAN

COLOGNE:
TONI SCHUMACHER · GERD STRACK · DIETER PRESTIN
HARALD KONOPKA · ROLAND GERBER · BERND CULLMANN
RENÉ BOTTERON · PIERRE LITTBARSKI · STEPHAN ENGELS
TONY WOODCOCK · DIETER MÜLLER
SUBS: HOLGER WILLMER · THOMAS KROTH

REFEREE: AUGUSTO LAMO CASTILLO (SPAIN)

**UEFA CUP WINNERS
1980/81
40TH ANNIVERSARY**

THE
semi
FINAL
FIRST LEG

FRANS THIJSSEN

JOHN WARK

After Ipswich had achieved such a magnificent victory over St-Étienne in the quarter-finals, few could have predicted the subsequent disastrous run of results leading up to the semi-final tie against Cologne that would see them lose their place at the top of Division One to Aston Villa. The run began with a 2-1 defeat at Manchester United and whilst a 4-1 victory over Sunderland at Portman Road helped settle nerves, further defeats at Leeds United and West Bromwich Albion put their title hopes in doubt.

Cologne were managed by Rinus Michels, a vastly-experienced coach who had previously enjoyed spells with Ajax and Barcelona as well as looking after the Dutch national team. Michels had assembled a formidable squad of top European players at Cologne, including English international striker Tony Woodcock, a £650,000 signing from Nottingham Forest.

However, they came into the game with key players nursing injuries and eventually Michels decided to leave skipper Rainer Bonhof and defender Herbert Zimmermann behind, but take a gamble on the fitness of full-back Gerd Strack. It was a decision that backfired almost immediately when the defender limped off the field with only five minutes on the clock.

Ipswich were enjoying the better of the early exchanges and they came within inches of opening the scoring when Thijssen sent in a low cross to the near post for Mariner to beat the defender to the ball, but his effort hit the foot of the post and was scrambled behind for a corner.

Soon afterwards they were close again after some great work by Gates out on the right. Brazil and Mills combined well before playing the ball up to Gates near the corner flag and even though he appeared to be closely marked, he turned his man to whip in a great cross which was headed narrowly wide of the far post by Wark. Then Thijssen was in with a chance when Mariner's through pass was deflected into his path, but the Dutchman's left-foot drive travelled wide.

It was even closer a few minutes later, and again it was Gates who created the opening, this time on the left when his pin-point cross picked out Brazil but the Scot's diving header travelled straight in the welcoming arms of Schumacher.

It had been all Ipswich in the first-half and on 38 minutes
they got their reward with yet another headed goal from Wark.

The flowing move down the right started in Town's own penalty area and involved Osman, Mills, Brazil and Gates before the ball was played wide to Mills who checked back to send in a superb left-foot cross for Wark to rise in typical fashion and send a magnificent downward header into the far corner of the net.

Wark's twelfth goal of the campaign brings European dream a step closer

A JUBILANT JOHN WARK & TERRY BUTCHER AFTER THE GAME

Just after the break the home side were in with a chance when a superb ball from Mühren sent Thijssen clear on the right, but Schumacher was off his line quickly to block the Dutchman's goal-bound effort. From the resulting corner Ipswich should have added a second when Butcher missed a great chance right in front of goal. Mühren took the kick and picked out Beattie at the far post who sent a looping header back into the six-yard box only for Butcher to head agonisingly wide with the goal gaping.

For the remainder of the second period the German side defended in depth, seemingly content to take a 1-0 defeat back home to Cologne for the second leg. Chances were few and far between as the game drew to a close, but at least Ipswich had kept a clean sheet, so important with away goals being so valuable in the competition. Nevertheless, it was the visiting players and their supporters who were celebrating at the final whistle.

Bobby Robson was philosophical about the result...

"**German teams are tough and difficult to beat. They defend well and give very little away, but at least it's a win and the tie is now finely balanced.**"

Unquestionably one of Bobby Robson's greatest signings for Ipswich Town and an absolute bargain at £150,000, Arnold Mühren made an instant impact at Portman Road where supporters voted him their Player of the Season in his first campaign with the club. Having previously played for Volendam and Ajax, Arnold was signed from FC Twente, and had already been capped by Holland when Bobby Robson clinched his signature in August 1978.

An elegant and stylish player with a magical left foot, Arnold possessed the rare ability to unlock defences with his vast array of passes and when Bobby Robson landed his former FC Twente teammate Frans Thijssen, the pair soon developed a devastating partnership in the heart of Town's midfield. The pair revolutionised Town's style of play and were virtually ever-presents in the 1980/81 season, by which time Arnold had also established himself as a key player in the Dutch national side.

Sadly, Arnold's time at Ipswich lasted only four years and in 1982, when his contract was up, Town were powerless to prevent him leaving on a free transfer. A number of clubs were in the hunt for his signature, but it was Manchester United that won the day. He enjoyed three great seasons at Old Trafford, and in 1985 he picked up an FA Cup-winners medal, converting a penalty in United's 4-0 victory over Brighton and Hove Albion. He was also a member of the United side that won the FA Charity Shield a few months later.

Soon afterwards Arnold returned to Holland to re-join Ajax where he added a European Cup Winners' Cup medal to his collection, and at the age of 37, he was a key member of the Dutch national team that lifted the European Championship in 1988. A year later, he finally hung up his boots to bring to an end a truly glorious career. He then teamed up with his brother Gerrie and the pair travelled the country coaching youngsters and teaching basic technique and passing skills.

Elected to Ipswich Town's Hall of Fame in 2009, Arnold Mühren will always be remembered as one of the greatest midfield players ever to grace the hallowed turf at Portman Road.

ARNOLD Mühren

PLAYER PROFILE

DATE OF BIRTH:	2 June 1951
PLACE OF BIRTH:	Volendam, Netherlands
IPSWICH TOWN:	214 Appearances · 29 Goals
1980/81 UEFA CUP:	12 Appearances · 1 Goal

FC COLOGNE 0

IPSWICH TOWN 1

Butcher (64)

Wednesday 22 April 1981
Müngersdorfer Stadion · Attendance: 55,000

COLOGNE:

TONI SCHUMACHER · DIETER PRESTIN · HARALD KONOPKA
BERND CULLMANN · HERBERT ZIMMERMANN · PIERRE LITTBARSKI
STEPHAN ENGELS · RENÉ BOTTERON · RAINER BONHOF
TONY WOODCOCK · DIETER MÜLLER · SUB USED: HOLGER WILLMER

IPSWICH TOWN:

PAUL COOPER · KEVIN STEGGLES · STEVE McCALL · FRANS THIJSSEN
RUSSELL OSMAN · TERRY BUTCHER · JOHN WARK · ARNOLD MÜHREN
PAUL MARINER · ALAN BRAZIL · MICK MILLS

REFEREE: KÁROLY PALOTAI (HUNGARY)

**UEFA CUP WINNERS
1980/81
40TH ANNIVERSARY**

THE
semi
FINAL
SECOND LEG

Ipswich could not have had a more daunting preparation for the second leg in Germany, having to play four huge games in less than two weeks, all of which would have a major impact on the outcome of their domestic campaign. The first, only three days after the first leg against Cologne, was a FA Cup semi-final against Manchester City at Villa Park. The game turned out to be a dour encounter which was goal-less at full time and for the first time in the history of the competition extra-time was played, much to the disappointment of the leg-weary Ipswich players who had lost Kevin Beattie in the closing stages of normal time with a broken arm.

The tie was eventually won by City with a stunning Paul Power free-kick and Town's treble dream was over. To make matters worse, although no-one knew it at the time, fans favourite Kevin Beattie would never play for the club again.

Three days later, Bobby Robson's team were back at Villa Park again, this time to face Aston Villa in what was billed by many as a title decider. Few pundits gave Town a chance given their gruelling schedule, but on the night they produced a magnificent performance with goals from Alan Brazil and Eric Gates securing a priceless 2-1 victory. Then, just when it looked as though their title hopes were back on track, they suffered two catastrophic defeats. The first was a 2-0 home defeat to Arsenal and then a single goal reverse in the East Anglian derby against Norwich City at Carrow Road on Easter Monday.

After the Norwich game, the dejected Ipswich party immediately travelled to Norwich Airport from where they flew out to Germany for the second leg against Cologne. Spirits were understandably low and in an attempt to lift morale, Bobby Robson stunned his players the day before the game by taking them to an amusement park on the outskirts of Cologne. It was fun and games all the way, particularly among the younger players who were allowed to let their hair down and relax in readiness for the game the following day.

John Wark recalls how well the Ipswich manager's pre-match tactics worked...

"After our recent disappointments on the domestic scene, the visit to the theme park certainly helped relax the lads and by the time the kick-off approached, we were really geared up for the challenge ahead. I'll always remember how keyed up our players were as we lined up in the tunnel, standing shoulder to shoulder with the Cologne players. Terry Butcher and Paul Mariner in particular were giving their players some real stick and by the look on their faces, you could sense we'd just won a major psychological battle."

WARK & THIJSSEN V MANCHESTER CITY

RUSSELL OSMAN CHALLENGES VILLA'S GARY SHAW

PAUL MARINER

With the tie so finely balanced, Bobby Robson decided to include an extra defender by recalling Kevin Steggles to the side and moving Mick Mills into a midfield role, replacing the unfortunate Eric Gates who had been injured in the home defeat to Arsenal. There was also a doubt over Paul Mariner's fitness and he was only able to play after receiving a pain-killing injection just before kick off and again at half-time.

The first goal was always going to be crucial and predictably perhaps, both managers adopted a cautious approach to the game particularly Cologne who were obviously aware that if Ipswich managed to grab an away goal, they would then need to score three.

However, the first real chance fell to the home side when they won a corner out on the right. The kick was taken short and when Konopka floated the ball in, Müller had a great chance right in front of goal, but his mistimed header travelled hopelessly wide. It was a bad miss, particularly for a player of his quality. Soon afterwards, Ipswich managed their first effort on target after great work by Mills on the left allowed Brazil and Mariner to combine and set up Wark, but his shot from about 20 yards was straight at Schumacher.

Then a right-wing cross was flicked on by Mariner to Brazil in a great position just inside the box, but the Ipswich striker was penalised for handling as he brought the ball under control. The play quickly switched to the opposite end where Botteron cut inside to unleash a powerful right-foot drive which was dealt with comfortably by Cooper. Then a beautifully weighted ball by Mühren sent Wark clear on goal, only for Schumacher to race from his line and make a great block.

The game was developing into a real end to end affair and on 30 minutes the home side missed another great chance when Konopka broke down the right to cross for Engels to head high and wide from a great position at the near post. Almost immediately they were back again and only a great tackle from Butcher prevented Müller getting through on goal.

The resulting corner was taken short for Botteron who picked out Cullmann racing into the box, but the defender sent his header flying over the bar, again from a great position. It had been a fairly even first half, but as the teams trooped off at the break, Cologne will no doubt have been rueing missing three presentable opportunities.

Needing to score to stay in the tie, Cologne begin the second period in the ascendancy and came close only a few minutes after the restart when the ball was played out to Konopka who unleashed a low right-foot shot that whipped across the six-yard box and just wide of the far post. Soon afterwards the home side came within a whisker of taking the lead when McCall's attempted back-pass fell short and only a brilliant stop by Cooper prevented Bonhof from opening the scoring.

Then, almost immediately, Brazil picked up a long ball out on the right and brilliantly turned two defenders to race into the box, but just as he was about to pull the trigger, Bonhof made a superb last-ditch sliding tackle to save the day. Throughout the game Ipswich had struggled to deal with the home side's aerial threat and on the hour Engels came within inches of making them pay when he headed a right-wing free-kick by Littbarski against the top of the upright with Cooper beaten all ends up.

At this stage Cologne looked the more likely team to break the deadlock, but on 64 minutes came the defining moment in the tie. From the start of the game Ipswich had adopted a positive approach, looking for that vital goal that would take the game out of Cologne's reach rather than hanging on to their slender first-leg lead. At every opportunity their defenders were lending their weight to the attack and they reaped the benefit when Butcher pushed forward after they had won a free-kick thirty yards from goal.

Mills took the kick and picked out the central-defender with a perfect cross which he headed low into the corner of the net, with a stunned Schumacher left rooted on his line. It was a great moment as Butcher raced away to celebrate, with his ecstatic teammates in hot pursuit, while on the bench Bobby Robson and Bobby Ferguson simply couldn't contain their joy.

Ipswich were now in total control and a few minutes later it should have been two when a brilliant turn by Brazil saw him break clear on the right. The striker raced to the by-line before pulling the ball back for Mills whose attempted shot fell perfectly into the path of the oncoming Wark, but his shot from only eight yards out flew over the bar.

Then in the final minute Engles, who had probably been Cologne's best player, broke through on the left to fire the ball across the face of the Ipswich goal with no-one able to get the vital touch.

TERRY BUTCHER SCORES

...AND CELEBRATES

Moments later, the final whistle blew and for the first time in their history, Ipswich Town had made it to a major European final and as their players and travelling supporters celebrated wildly, the dejected Cologne players trooped off the pitch.

In particular, Alan Brazil had put in an outstanding performance up front by undertaking the lion's share of the front-running duties due to Paul Mariner carrying an injury. He recalled...

"That was my kind of game. I really enjoyed it, despite the fact that I was tired about fifteen minutes from the end. I just tried to put the tiredness to the back of my mind and not let it affect me."

At the final whistle goalscorer Terry Butcher was besieged by the press who were desperate to hear his take on his match-winning goal.

"I couldn't believe it," said Butcher, **"When I headed the ball, I was certain it was going wide but at the last second it hit the ground and curled into the corner of the net just clipping the inside of the post on it's way!"**

Bobby Robson's tactics had proved to be spot on and whilst they rode their luck at times, his team finished the game as worthy winners. After the match a delighted Town manager was full of praise for his team...

"We've revived ourselves and played the game with a lot of spirit just like we did after we lost to Manchester City in the FA Cup semi-final and then went to Aston Villa and won. Great defensive play here, but on the break we got players forward in good numbers and I think we played splendidly and deserved to win. I knew that they would push people forward, and they only played two at the back which suited Mariner and Brazil, and the ball into space was always on. We felt we had to score, and to defend and defend was always going to be a risk. We've done it and I'm just delighted for all the people at Ipswich!"

As the Ipswich party left the stadium, news came through that their opponents in the final would be Dutch side AZ '67 Alkmaar who had just defeated FC Sochaux 4-3 on aggregate in the other semi-final. Like Ipswich, they were also chasing their domestic league championship and faced key games in the two weeks leading up the first leg of the final at Portman Road.

ALAN BRAZIL SHAKES HANDS
WITH COLOGNE'S RAINER BONHOF

Son of former Derby County player Rex Osman, Russell always seemed destined to a career in the top-class game and he actually picked up an FA Youth Cup winners medal with Ipswich in 1975 while still studying at his school in Derbyshire.

His elevation to first-team football at Portman Road came just over two years later in a 1-0 victory over Chelsea and whilst he went on to make 38 league and cup appearances that season, he was desperately unlucky not to make an appearance in the 1978 FA Cup-winning team.

Thereafter, he was pretty much a fixture in the side, establishing a formidable partnership with Terry Butcher at the heart of the Ipswich Town defence. A solid and dependable two-footed player, Russell was a hard-tackling defender who was equally effective in the air and, having already represented England at youth and Under-21 level, it came as no surprise when full international honours arrived.

He won his first cap in a friendly international against Australia on 31 May 1980 when he played alongside Town colleagues, Terry Butcher, Brian Talbot and Paul Mariner in a 2-1 victory. Russell eventually went on to win a total of eleven full caps for his country.

Noted for his consistent performances, Russell was the only player to appear in all 66 games in Town's remarkable 1980/81 campaign, his second consecutive season as an ever-present. In all he made almost 400 appearances for the club before joining Leicester City for £200,000 in August 1985 where he enjoyed three highly successful seasons before moving to the south coast to join Southampton. The 1995/96 season saw Russell enjoy brief spells with Brighton and Hove Albion and Cardiff City before bringing his playing career to a close.

After hanging up his boots, he moved into coaching and then management with first Bristol City and then Cardiff City. Then in 2015 he joined Newport County as assistant manager to former Ipswich Town colleague Terry Butcher, although his spell with the Welsh club was one of disappointment and lasted only a few months.

Inducted into the Ipswich Town Hall of Fame in 2011, Russell was also one of a number of Town players who appeared in the 1981 film 'Escape to Victory' in which he played Doug Clure, one of the prisoner-of-war footballers.

OSMAN IN FA CUP SEMI-FINAL ACTION V MANCHESTER CITY

OSMAN HEADS CLEAR FROM LIVERPOOL'S KENNY DALGLISH

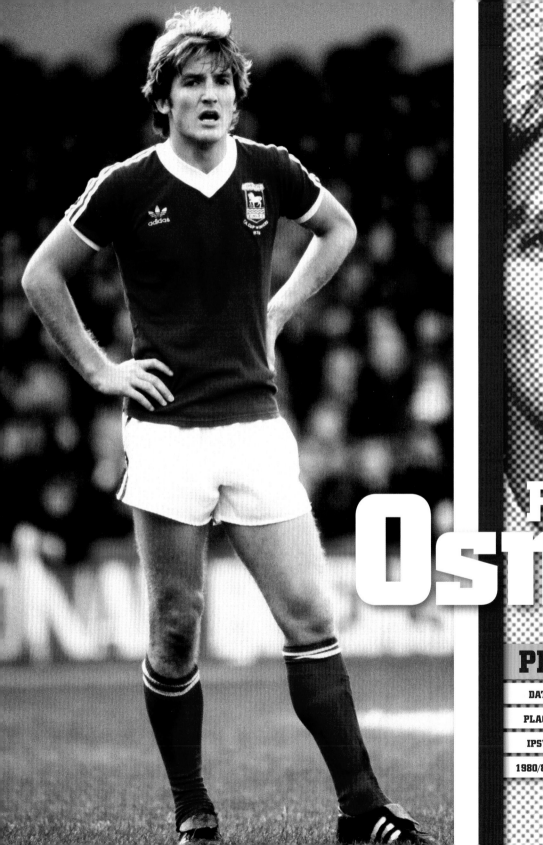

RUSSELL Osman

PLAYER PROFILE

DATE OF BIRTH:	14 February 1959
PLACE OF BIRTH:	Repton, Derbyshire
IPSWICH TOWN:	385 Appearances · 21 Goals
1980/81 UEFA CUP:	12 Appearances

IPSWICH TOWN

UEFA CUP FINAL
First leg
Wednesday, May 6th 1981
Kick-off 7.30 p.m.

AZ'67 Alkmaar

Official
Match Day
Magazine
Price 30p.

TONIGHT'S MATCH SPONSORS

contship

IPSWICH TOWN 3

Wark (28 Pen), Thijssen (46), Mariner (56)

AZ'67 ALKMAAR 0

Wednesday 6 May 1981
Portman Road · Attendance: 27,532

IPSWICH TOWN:

PAUL COOPER · MICK MILLS · STEVE McCALL · FRANS THIJSSEN
RUSSELL OSMAN · TERRY BUTCHER · JOHN WARK · ARNOLD MÜHREN
PAUL MARINER · ALAN BRAZIL · ERIC GATES

AZ'67 ALKMAAR:

EDDY TREIJTEL · RICHARD VAN DER MEER · RONALD SPELBOS
JOHN METGOD · HUGO HOVENKAMP · JAN PETERS · JOS JONKER
PETER ARNTZ · PIER TOL · KEES KIST · KRISTEN NYGAARD
SUB USED: KURT WELZL

REFEREE: ADOLF PROKOP (EAST GERMANY)

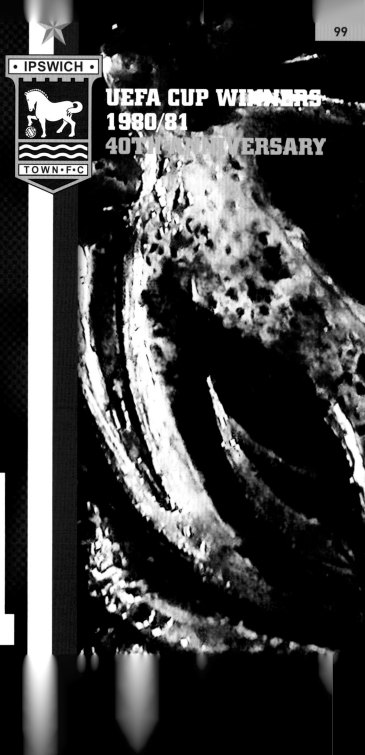

**UEFA CUP WINNERS
1980/81
40TH ANNIVERSARY**

THE final

Bobby Robson and his team were afforded very little time to savour their semi-final victory in Cologne as attention almost immediately turned to the vital home game against Manchester City at Portman Road just three days later. Despite their recent poor run of results Ipswich were still very much in the running for the league title and they kept their hopes alive with a crucial 1-0 victory and also exacted some revenge for their FA Cup semi-final defeat at the hands of City a few weeks earlier. Again Terry Butcher was the match-winner netting the only goal of the game.

Ipswich were now four points behind league leaders Aston Villa, but crucially had played one game less. If Villa failed to win their final game, away to Arsenal, and Ipswich won their two remaining fixtures, away to Middlesbrough and then at home to Southampton, then the title was almost certainly theirs due to their superior goal difference.

For Ipswich Town fans of a certain generation the afternoon of the 2 May 1981 will undoubtedly live long in the memory and can without doubt be described as an emotional rollercoaster of epic proportions. Many of those supporters had travelled up to Teesside and packed the Ayresome Park terraces hoping to see their team take a further step towards the ultimate prize whilst also keeping a close watch on events taking place at Highbury where top of the league Villa were taking on Arsenal.

The game began brilliantly for Bobby Robson's team who dominated the first half with Paul Mariner's goal giving them a half time lead, and when the news filtered through that Villa were losing 2-0 at Highbury, the odds appeared to be swinging in Town's favour. However, their dreams would soon be shattered by two second-half goals from Middlesbrough's Yugoslav striker Boško Janković and despite incessant pressure in the closing stages, they couldn't conjure up an equaliser. To make matters worse, the news filtered through that Villa had lost at Arsenal, but with their four point lead over Ipswich still intact the title was theirs.

To come so close after such a marvellous season was a devastating blow for everyone associated with Ipswich Town Football Club and as they headed back to Suffolk, Bobby Robson now faced one of the toughest challenges of his managerial career knowing that he had only four days to lift the spirits of his squad for the UEFA Cup final first leg at Portman Road. By contrast their opponents, AZ'67 Alkmaar, were celebrating a resounding 5-1 win at Feyenoord, a victory that saw them clinch the Dutch Championship.

The long, hard season had certainly taken its toll on Robson's players, many of whom had played in games when they simply weren't fully fit. This was largely due to the fact that Town's relatively small squad lacked any real strength in depth making it almost impossible for the Ipswich boss to rest any of his key players during the hectic run-in at the end of the campaign.

After the disappointment of missing out on the treble, it was time for the whole club to focus on the UEFA Cup final.

JOHN WARK HEADS FOR GOAL WITH TERRY BUTCHER IN ATTENDANCE

PAUL MARINER GETS IN A HEADER ON GOAL

Nevertheless, he was able to name a full-strength team for the first leg of the final as they were about to embark on arguably the biggest game in the history of the club. Many in the media had predicted that Ipswich simply wouldn't be able to rise to the challenge given their disappointment at missing out on the league title, although after watching Town's victory over Manchester City the AZ'67 Alkmaar coach, Georg Keßler, had a differing view stating…

"Ipswich are a team of power, they like to attack and they are entertaining. They must be favourites for the UEFA Cup. I would say that Ipswich and AZ have played the best football in Europe this season. I am not surprised they have reached the UEFA Cup final, in fact they are good enough for the European Cup final."

Dutch Master Thijssen doubles the Blues lead early in the second half

AZ'67 Alkmaar had a reputation for playing flowing, attacking football, yet the Ipswich fans that packed into Portman Road were soon seeing another, more physical side to their game as the tackles flew in virtually from the kick-off. The Dutch champions, whose side included numerous top international players, seemed more intent on employing spoiling tactics rather than playing the entertaining brand of football for which Dutch teams had become so famous.

Predictably, Ipswich began in the ascendancy looking for that all-important early goal and they came close after only eight minutes with a great effort from Gates. Picking up the ball in his own half, the Ipswich winger went on a great run through the middle and played a one-two with Brazil before unleashing a vicious right-foot shot from outside the box which had Treijtel diving low to his right to turn the effort around the post.

Ipswich were enjoying the lion's share of possession, but the Dutch champions were proving difficult to break down. However, the breakthrough came just before the half-hour mark with a move started on the right by Mills whose left-foot cross was flicked on by Mühren to Wark racing into the box. Although tightly marked the Ipswich midfielder managed to flick the ball across the face of the goal to Mariner who sent in a right-foot volley which was handled on the line by Hovenkamp and referee Prokop had no hesitation in pointing to the spot.

John Wark had already netted four penalties in the competition and again the Scot made no mistake sending the 'keeper the wrong way with a powerful right-foot shot low into the corner of the net. Soon afterwards the home side could have doubled their advantage when Wark found Thijssen who surged through the middle into a great position only to see his left-foot shot travel wide of the post.

In the first half little had been seen of the Dutch champions as an attacking force and they were probably more than happy to return to the dressing room with only a one goal deficit given the home side's dominance.

However, the whole complexion of the game would change immediately after the break when Thijssen netted number two on 46 minutes following a great passing move started by Butcher in his own half. McCall, Mariner, Gates and Brazil were all involved before the ball was played through to Thijssen racing into the right side of the box and when his right-foot shot was blocked by Treijtel the ball spun into the air for the Dutchman to follow up and head the ball into the empty net.

By now Portman Road really was rocking as the home side pressed forward looking to drive home their advantage and they nearly added a third after great work by Mariner and Brazil saw Gates send in a terrific dipping shot that just cleared the bar.

Soon afterwards however, the third goal duly arrived and again it was the result of a fine passing move down the left started by Cooper's throw-out and ending with Brazil turning his man brilliantly before sending in a low cross to the near post that was flicked home by Paul Mariner.

With the tie now appearing to be slipping from their grasp, AZ began to press forward looking for the vital away goal that would resurrect their hopes and with ten minutes remaining they almost got it. Welzl, who had replaced Nygaard earlier in the half, broke down the right to send in a terrific cross to pick out Tol just inside the box, but the Dutchman's left-foot volley flew high and wide.

Then in the dying seconds Metgod evaded Mühren's challenge to get to the by-line and pull the ball back to Kist but his right-foot shot flew over the bar. It was a bad miss by the Dutch international striker and moments later the final whistle blew to signal a momentous victory for Bobby Robson's team who left the field to a standing ovation from their ecstatic fans.

In the dressing room their delighted manager congratulated each of his players on a truly outstanding performance and commented...

"We played as well tonight as we have done all season, I think we murdered them. We played at a pace that they couldn't master and couldn't keep at. All right, we drifted a bit in the last ten minutes but that was due to the number of games we've played this season and we were a little bit weary at the end. Thijssen and Mariner who haven't trained recently probably felt the pace more than the others, but prodigious efforts by them and everybody else of course. I hope we've made history for the club because it's been a long time coming but we still have a bit to do in Amsterdam because it's not going to be easy."

"In my opinion we've been the best team in the country this season and I think we proved it tonight."

ALAN BRAZIL, ARNOLD MÜHREN, FRANS THIJSSEN AND PAUL MARINER JUBILANT AT REACHING THE FINAL

When Frans Thijssen arrived at Portman Road in February 1979 he was able to restore his midfield partnership with Arnold Mühren, his former colleague at FC Twente. It was actually Mühren that persuaded Town manager Bobby Robson to make a move for his fellow Dutchman and the pair wasted no time in taking the English game by storm, resulting in Thijssen being named 'Player of the Year' by Town supporters in his first full season at the club.

A hugely-talented player with great balance and the ability to destroy the opposition with his mazy runs, Frans was the final piece in the jigsaw as Robson assembled what many regard as Ipswich Town's greatest ever team.

He was a key player in the 1980/81 UEFA Cup-winning side including scoring twice in the final against AZ'67 Alkmaar and capped a great campaign by being named the football writer's Footballer of the Year, only the second foreign recipient of the prestigious award. His outstanding form for Town also prompted Dutch manager Jan Zwartkruis to recall Frans to the national side, and he eventually went on to win a total of fourteen caps for his country.

In all, Frans spent four years at Portman Road before being signed by Nottingham Forest manager Brian Clough, but he rarely hit the heights at the City Ground and his stay lasted little more than a few months. He then headed out to Canada to try his luck with Vancouver Whitecaps, but after only one season he returned to his homeland to join Fortuna Sittard. In 1991, after spells with FC Groningen and Vitesse Arnhem, Frans finally brought his playing career to a close and moved into management.

In 1997, he was appointed a manager of Swedish club Malmö FF, but in 1998, after two years without success and with the club in danger of being relegated for the first time in their history, he and the club parted ways. Frans then returned to the Netherlands where he had brief spells in charge at De Graafschap and his former club Fortuna Sittard before heading out to Australia to take over as caretaker-manager of Brisbane Roar.

Frans Thijssen was one of the most talented players ever to grace Portman Road and in 2008 he received the ultimate accolade when he was inducted into Ipswich Town's 'Hall of Fame'.

THIJSSEN WEAVES HIS WAY THROUGH THE LIVERPOOL DEFENCE

FRANS Thijssen

PLAYER PROFILE

DATE OF BIRTH:	23 January 1952
PLACE OF BIRTH:	Malden, Netherlands
IPSWICH TOWN:	170 Appearances · 16 Goals
1980/81 UEFA CUP:	10 Appearances · 2 Goals

AZ'67 ALKMAAR 4

Welzl (7), Metgod (24), Tol (39), Jonker (73)

IPSWICH TOWN 2

Thijssen (4), Wark (31)

Wednesday 20 May 1981
Olympisch Stadion, Amsterdam · Attendance: 28,500

AZ'67 ALKMAAR:
EDDY TREIJTEL · HANS REIJNDERS · RONALD SPELBOS
JOHN METGOD · HUGO HOVENKAMP · JAN PETERS
JOS JONKER · PETER ARNTZ · KURT WELZL · KRISTEN NYGAARD
PIER TOL · SUBS USED: KEES KIST · RICK TALAN

IPSWICH TOWN:
PAUL COOPER · MICK MILLS · STEVE McCALL · FRANS THIJSSEN
RUSSELL OSMAN · TERRY BUTCHER · JOHN WARK
ARNOLD MÜHREN · PAUL MARINER · ALAN BRAZIL · ERIC GATES

REFEREE: WALTER ESCHWEILER (WEST GERMANY)

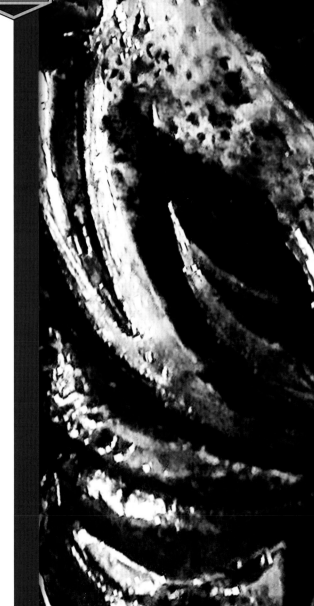

IPSWICH

TOWN·F·C

**UEFA CUP WINNERS
1980/81
40TH ANNIVERSARY**

THE
final
SECOND LEG

More than 7,000 fans travelled across the North Sea for the second leg, confident that they were about to see their team lift its first-ever European trophy. Certainly the odds were stacked heavily in favour of Ipswich, but they were about to encounter a dramatic game that would have their supporters on the edge of their seats right to the very end.

SKIPPER MICK MILLS LEADS OUT HIS BLUES TEAM

One-Nil
after only four minutes

FRANS THIJSSEN IS MOBBED BY DELIGHTED TEAMMATES

Bobby Robson fielded the same team that had won so convincingly in the first leg with AZ making one change, Hans Reijnders coming in at right back in place of Richard van der Meer.

Any suggestions that Ipswich would rest on their laurels and defend from the start were soon dispelled when they stormed into the lead after only four minutes. The goal came from a left-wing corner taken by Gates and when the ball was headed out by Arntz, it landed perfectly for Thijssen on the edge of the box who sent in a superb right-foot volley that flew into the corner of the net with Treijtel left rooted to his line.

It was a dream start for Robson's men, and their supporters celebrated in style as their own rendition of 'You'll Never Walk Alone' reverberated around the stadium, but if they thought the tie was over, they were in for a rude awakening as the home side hit back almost immediately.

Metgod was the architect of the goal, picking up a through ball inside the box and when Cooper forced him wide, he turned to float in a great cross that was headed home by Welzl from close range. Sensing that they might still be able to find a way back into the game, the Dutch side surged forward and after eight minutes they missed a great opportunity to add to their score.

The ball was played into the Ipswich box and when it was blocked, Metgod miscued his shot only to see the ball fall invitingly for Jonker on the edge of the six-yard box. It looked a certain goal, but the Dutch midfielder somehow managed to drive his effort onto the top the bar from point blank range with the home crowd already celebrating.

AZ continued to pour forward in their droves with Ipswich struggling to get possession and having to rely on some desperate defending to keep them at bay. However, in a rare breakaway they almost regained the lead when a long kick by Cooper was flicked on by Mariner to send Brazil in on goal, but his right-foot effort from the edge of the box was well saved by Treijtel. Soon afterwards, Mariner brilliantly beat his man on the right touchline and raced down the wing before crossing to Thijssen in space on the edge of the box, only for the Dutchman's attempted pass to Gates at the far post to be cut out by Hovenkamp.

At last, Ipswich were beginning to get a foothold in the game and on 19 minutes they created another opportunity after winning a free-kick just inside the AZ half. Mills took the kick quickly and sent Mariner away down the right wing and when his cross from the bye-line was headed down by Wark, Gates had a great chance from the edge of the box, but his right-foot volley flew high over the bar.

On 24 minutes, the home side were right back in the tie when they took the lead with a terrific header by Metgod. The move began down the right with Peters getting to the bye-line to whip in a vicious cross for Metgod to rise above Osman and head home from the edge of the six-yard box giving Cooper in the Ipswich goal no chance.

Sensing that AZ might now have a real chance of the saving the tie, the home supporters suddenly came to life and got right behind their team. Within minutes they were almost celebrating a third goal when an intricate passing move ended with Peters shooting into the side netting from a great position to the right of goal.

Then, following a long kick by Cooper, the ball was played out to Brazil on the left and when he beat his man and cut inside, he unleashed a low right-foot drive that was well saved by Treijtel at the foot of the near post. The Blues came even closer soon afterwards when they won a free-kick after Brazil was fouled 25 yards from goal. Mühren took the kick and curled in a beautiful left-foot shot towards the top corner only for Treijtel to pull off a brilliant save.

The next goal was clearly going to be crucial and fortunately for the travelling hordes from Suffolk, it was their team that got it and again it was John Wark who delivered right on cue. The goal came from a right-wing corner taken by Mühren which was headed on by Mariner at the near post for Wark to volley home from close range. It was the Scottish international's 14th goal of the UEFA Cup campaign, an amazing record for a midfielder, equalling the record in European competition set by AC Milan's Jose Altafini 18 year previous.

As the Ipswich players celebrated in front of the fans it seemed that surely there was no way back for the home side yet once again they responded in magnificent fashion.

Pressing forward in numbers, they came close when Metgod sent in a thumping low drive that was well saved by Cooper. From the resulting clearance, Wark sprung the offside trap only to be thwarted by Treijtel who raced from the penalty area to punch clear, much to the annoyance of the Ipswich players who felt the AZ 'keeper should have been booked. Mühren took the free-kick to send Butcher down the right and his low cross was knocked back in by Gates on the opposite flank only to be cut out by Treijtel.

Wark's 14th goal of the UEFA Cup campaign settles the nerves, for now...

A nervous looking Blues bench...

It had been a truly amazing first half of end-to-end attacking football and with only six minutes remaining, AZ gave themselves an unlikely life-line to take into the break. The influential Metgod was again involved, heading on Peters' cross to Jonker and when the ball dropped at the far post, Tol stepped in to beat Cooper all ends up with a crisp low right-foot drive.

Then, following a scramble on the edge of the Ipswich box, Jonker unleashed a rising drive that flew over the bar with Cooper at full stretch. As the players trooped off at half-time Ipswich were still very much in control, yet back in the dressing room Bobby Robson will have no doubt been impressing on them that the tie was far from over.

At the break, AZ made one tactical change bringing on their Dutch international striker Kees Kist in place of Pier Tol as they attempted to conjure up the goals that might swing the tie in their favour. Kist was soon in the thick of the action and on 55 minutes he unleashed a powerful 25-yard shot that Cooper dealt with comfortably. With the home side pressing forward relentlessly Ipswich were now sitting much deeper, relying on the strong running of Brazil and Mariner up front to ease the pressure. However, time and again their progress was halted when they were caught offside as the AZ back line pushed forward almost up to the half-way line.

Despite the home side enjoying the lion's share of possession, the Ipswich defence were dealing with their pressure without problem and the best opportunity of the second half actually fell to the visitors. Mariner won the ball on the half-way line and set off on a run for goal only to see his long-range effort fly over the bar.

The Ipswich defence had been largely untroubled in the second period, but on 67 minutes, only a truly stunning save from Cooper prevented the home side from reducing the deficit. A long cross-field ball was picked up by Peters on the right touchline and when he beat McCall on the outside he whipped in a great cross for Welzl to send a terrific header from only a few yards out. It looked a certain goal, but Cooper somehow managed to leap acrobatically and claw the ball clear from right under the crossbar. It was a truly breathtaking save of pure world-class quality.

Undeterred, the home side continued to press forward in numbers, but midway through the half. Ipswich came close to grabbing an equaliser when Wark drove through the middle before unleashing a great left-foot shot that just cleared the bar.

The massed ranks of Ipswich fans now began to sense victory with chants of 'We're going to win the Cup' and 'You'll Never Walk Alone' getting louder and louder as the game wore on.

TOM PARKIN (MADE FOUR LEAGUE APPEARANCES DURING 1980/81, BUT DID NOT APPEAR IN ANY UEFA CUP GAMES), KEVIN O'CALLAGHAN, ROBIN TURNER, BOBBY ROBSON & CHARLIE WOODS

However, with only 17 minutes remaining they were suddenly silenced when AZ 67 netted a fourth goal to put the game on a knife edge. The goal came from a free-kick when Butcher was penalised for a shuddering challenge that sent Metgod flying to the ground, and when Jonker stepped up, he sent a thunderous drive through the defensive wall and high into the corner of the net giving Cooper no chance.

This incredible game was now set for a grand finale as the home side, roared on by their fanatical fans, began to lay siege on the Ipswich goal looking for the goal that would level the aggregate score. With ten minutes remaining they almost got it when Peters cut in from the right to curl in a left-foot shot, but the effort was well saved by Cooper diving low to his right. Brazil had worked tirelessly up front, holding up the ball to ease the pressure on the Ipswich defence and after one particular run down the left he laid the ball back for Mühren to swing in a terrific left-foot cross which picked out Wark on a typical run, but his header at the far post travelled well wide.

As the game moved into the final minutes, the home side were now resorting to throwing long balls into the box which were dealt with comfortably by the Ipswich defence that had performed magnificently throughout the second half. By now the Ipswich fans were in full voice and at the final whistle many poured onto the pitch to congratulate their heroes. At last, after such a gruelling campaign and so many disappointments on the domestic front, they had managed to lift arguably the most coveted prize of all - the club's first-ever European trophy.

Looking back on what he regarded as his finest moment in club football, Bobby Robson was also generous in his praise of AZ 67 Alkmaar and acknowledged how difficult the second leg had been for his team...

"I have to give great credit to their German coach Georg Keßler for how he approached the game. With nothing to lose, they set out to attack the game and played just two at the back against Mariner and Brazil. They threw everybody forward and it was a whirlwind. They were unrelenting, played wonderful attacking football and we just couldn't get the ball. But we hung in there and with the cushion of that one goal, they couldn't beat us. It was a wonderful end to a marvellous season, but for me, the pleasure was for everybody else; the players, our supporters and the wonderful people of Ipswich."

A JUBILANT BOBBY ROBSON AT THE FINAL WHISTLE

MICK MILLS ABOUT TO BE PRESENTED WITH THE UEFA CUP

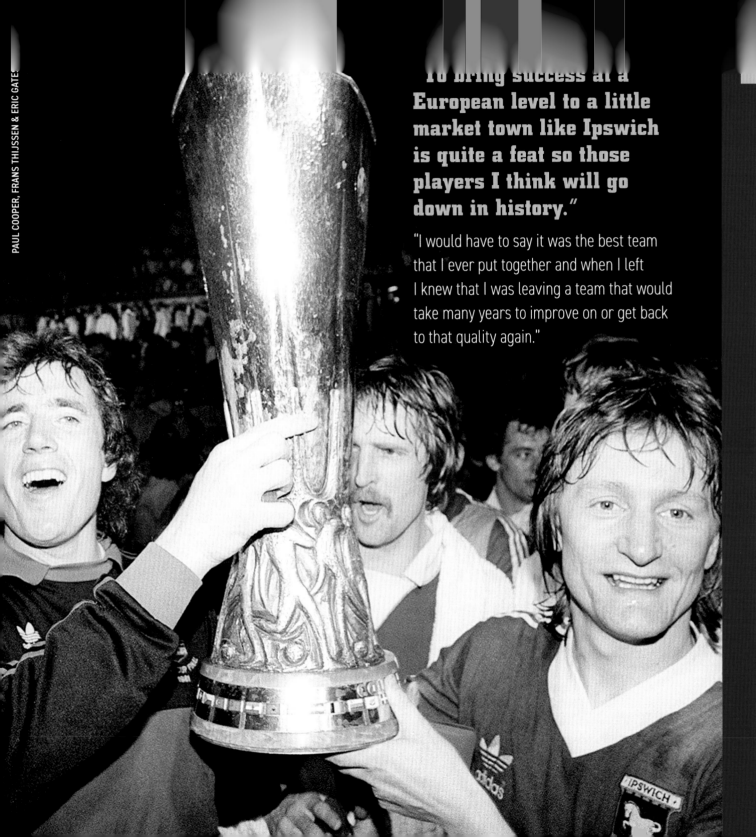

To bring success at a European level to a little market town like Ipswich is quite a feat so those players I think will go down in history."

"I would have to say it was the best team that I ever put together and when I left I knew that I was leaving a team that would take many years to improve on or get back to that quality again."

Dagenham-born Kevin O'Callaghan began his career in football in 1977 as an apprentice with Millwall and quickly developed through the ranks before making his debut in league football the following season. A talented left-winger, Kevin began to attract the attention of a number of First Division clubs before Bobby Robson eventually clinched his signature during the 1980 close season.

After making his debut in a 4-0 victory over Everton at Goodison Park in February 1980, Kevin went on to make 35 appearances for Town during the 1980/81 season although the majority of these were substitute appearances including five during the UEFA Cup run.

He remained very much a fringe player during the following season, but enjoyed regular first-team football thereafter, going on to make 147 appearances for the club. In November 1982, Kevin was called up by Republic of Ireland manager Eoin Hand and picked up his first full international cap in the 3-3 draw with Spain in the European Championship qualifiers at Lansdowne Road, Dublin. He went on to win 21 caps for his country.

Kevin was also one of the Ipswich Town players who appeared in the feature film 'Escape to Victory' starring Michael Caine and Sylvester Stallone that was filmed in Hungary in 1980, before hitting the big screen the following year. Apart from the Ipswich Town players, the film also featured numerous other football stars including Pelé, Bobby Moore, Ossie Ardiles and Mike Summerbee. Kevin's character in the film was Tony Lewis who volunteered to have his arm broken so that Hatch, played by Stallone, could be freed from solitary confinement.

His career at Portman Road lasted until 1985 when he joined Portsmouth and in 1987 he helped his new club clinch promotion back to the First Division. He then returned to Millwall where he was a key figure in the Lions team that made it to the top flight for the first time in their history in 1988.

Kevin then enjoyed a two-year spell with Southend United before a severe knee injury brought his playing career to an abrupt end during the 1992/93 season. He then moved into coaching, eventually returning to Millwall where he helped to produce a procession of talented youngsters.

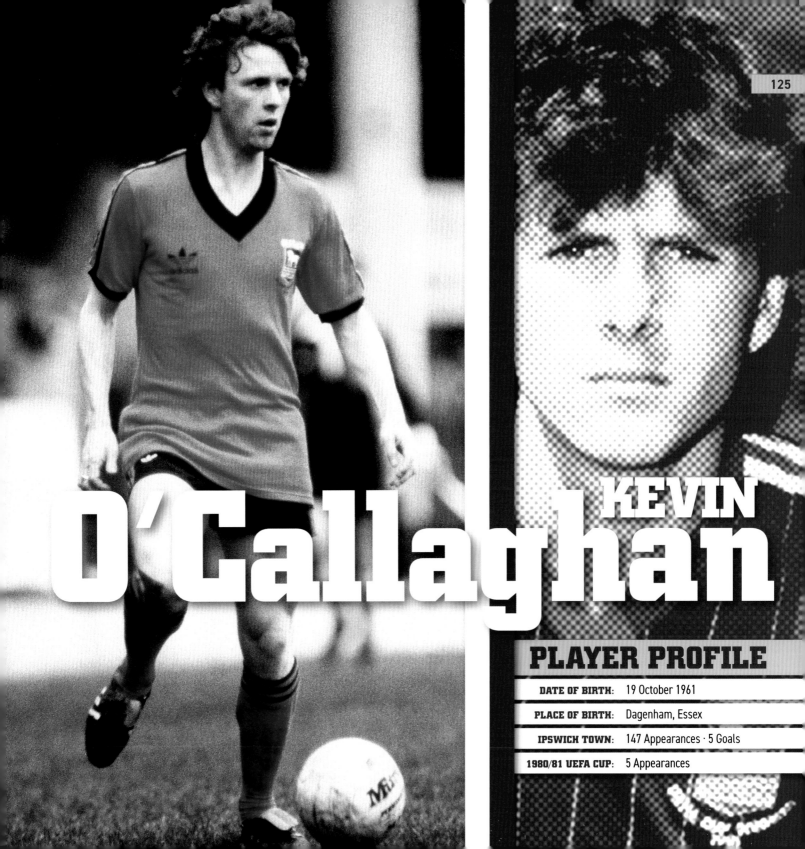

KEVIN O'Callaghan

PLAYER PROFILE

DATE OF BIRTH:	19 October 1961
PLACE OF BIRTH:	Dagenham, Essex
IPSWICH TOWN:	147 Appearances · 5 Goals
1980/81 UEFA CUP:	5 Appearances

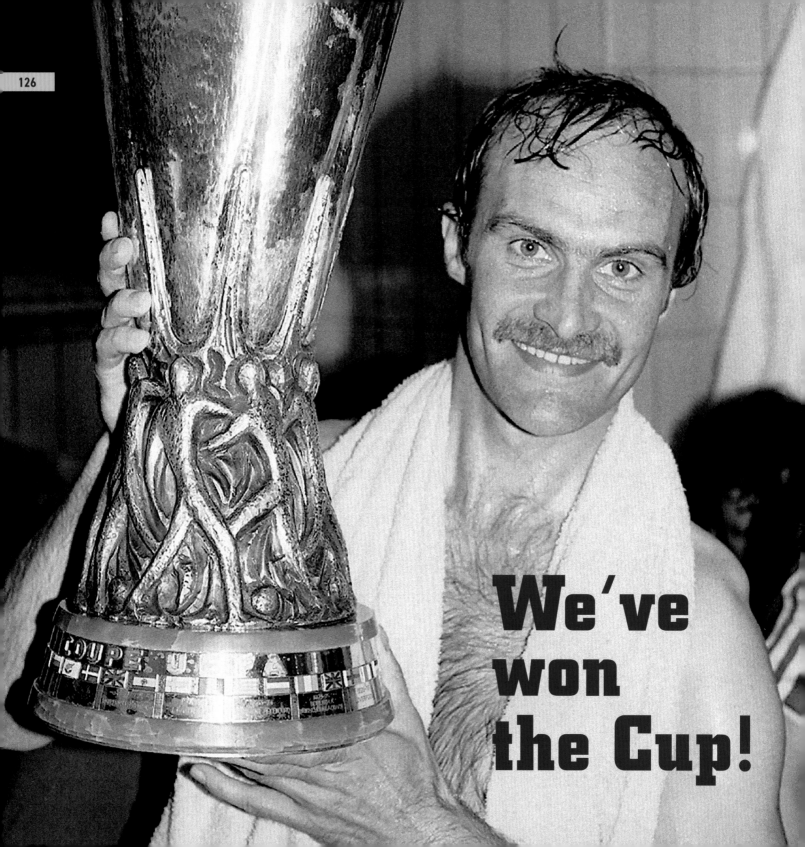

We've won the Cup!

The only member of Ipswich Town's 1980/81 UEFA Cup-winning team not to be signed by Bobby Robson, Mick Mills joined the club as a youngster from Portsmouth when the Fratton Park club scrapped their youth set-up in February 1966. Mick made his first-team debut a few months later in the final home game of the season against Wolverhampton Wanderers, thus began a truly brilliant Portman Road career that would span over sixteen years during which he would make a record 741 appearances for the club.

Equally at home at full-back or midfield, he was appointed captain by Bobby Robson in 1971, quickly developing into an inspirational leader, as Ipswich soon became one of the leading contenders for the League title. While that prize proved to be somewhat elusive, Mick had the honour of becoming the first Town player to lift the FA Cup following their 1-0 victory over Arsenal in 1978, a year that also saw him voted Player of the Year by Town supporters.

By then the Ipswich skipper was an established England international having been handed his first full cap by Sir Alf Ramsey during the 1972/73 season in a 1-1 draw with Yugoslavia at Wembley, the first of 42 appearances for his country. Those appearances included five in the 1982 World Cup finals in Spain where he enjoyed the honour of captaining his country throughout the tournament.

Whilst his dream of lifting the English League championship never materialised, Mick could take comfort in lifting the UEFA Cup in 1981, the first and to date, the only Ipswich captain to lift a major European trophy. Mick's long and illustrious Ipswich Town career came to an end in 1982 when he was somewhat surprisingly sold to Southampton for what appeared to be a ridiculously low fee of £40,000. He spent three seasons at The Dell before joining Stoke City as player-manager during the 1985 close-season, going on to make over 40 appearances for the Potteries club before hanging up his boots at the age of 38 to concentrate on the management side of the game.

Sadly, Mick's time in charge at Stoke became a constant struggle against relegation and in November 1989, with the club rooted at the bottom of Division Two and heading for English football's third tier for the first time ever, it came as no surprise when he was relieved of his duties. He later had a brief and unsuccessful spell in charge at Colchester and also served Birmingham City and Sheffield Wednesday in a coaching capacity before finally retiring from the game in December 2001.

In January 1984, Mick was awarded an MBE for his services to football and in 2007 he was inducted into Ipswich Town's Hall of Fame, a fitting tribute to one of Portman Road's all-time greats.

ENGLAND 1982 WORLD CUP CAPTAIN

MICK Mills

PLAYER PROFILE

DATE OF BIRTH: 4 January 1949

PLACE OF BIRTH: Godalming, Surrey

IPSWICH TOWN: 741 Appearances · 30 Goals

1980/81 UEFA CUP: 10 Appearances

When Bobby Robson and his conquering heroes returned home to Ipswich they were greeted with truly incredible scenes as the quiet Suffolk town seemed to be engulfed in UEFA Cup fever.

A special civic reception had been arranged by the Borough Council which, in recognition of such a magnificent season, would have gone ahead even if Town had lost the final.

The whole town seemed to be bathed in blue and white as the open-topped bus carrying the cup-winning squad set off from Portman Road and inched its way though the crowds lining the route to the town centre that were estimated to be in the region of 50,000.

MICK MILLS & BOBBY ROBSON

Kevin STEGGLES

Laurie SIVELL

Few players can have had a more daunting first-team debut than 19-year-old Kevin Steggles who was asked to stand in for the injured Mick Mills in Town's 1980/81 UEFA Cup quarter-final, second leg tie against St-Étienne. Not only that, he was then given the task marking Dutch international star Johnny Rep, one of Europe's finest players at the time. Nevertheless, the Ipswich youngster stuck to his task brilliantly and the fact that the Dutchman barely had a kick during the game stands testament to Kevin's defensive qualities.

Kevin also played in Town's semi-final second-leg victory over Cologne and having produced another excellent display was perhaps a little unfortunate not to be included in Bobby Robson's squad for the final against AZ'67 Alkmaar.

The following season saw Kevin enjoy the best campaign of his Ipswich career when he made 22 appearances in all competitions, but in the years that followed he was very much on the fringes of the first team. In 1987, after loan spells with Southend United and Fulham, he severed his ties with the club to join West Bromwich Albion. Kevin's stay at the Hawthorns lasted only one season and in 1987, he signed for Port Vale before finally ending his career in league football at the end of the 1987/88 season and moving into non-league football.

Originally spotted playing local football in Lowestoft, Laurie Sivell spent 15 years at Portman Road after joining the club as a 17-year-old in 1969. Although relatively small for a goalkeeper, Kevin more than made up for his lack of inches with his superb agility and braveness, often denying opposition by throwing himself at the feet of their oncoming forwards.

Laurie made his first-team debut in a 2-0 defeat against Liverpool at Anfield in March 1970 and went on to make a more than respectable 175 appearances for the club which surely would have been much greater, but for the superb form of Paul Cooper.

Laurie managed only one appearance during the 1980/81 UEFA Cup campaign, standing in the injured Paul Cooper in the second round, second leg tie against Bohemians in Prague. In freezing temperatures, Town managed a narrow 3-2 aggregate victory due largely to a magnificent rearguard action that saw Laurie make a number of vital saves.

He retired from the game in 1984 and, apart from two games while on loan at Lincoln City in 1979, Ipswich Town was his only league club.

PLAYER PROFILE

DATE OF BIRTH:	19 March 1961
PLACE OF BIRTH:	Ditchingham, Norfolk
IPSWICH TOWN:	61 Appearances · 2 Goals
1980/81 UEFA CUP:	2 Appearances

PLAYER PROFILE

DATE OF BIRTH:	6 February 1951
PLACE OF BIRTH:	Lowestoft, Suffolk
IPSWICH TOWN:	175 Appearances
1980/81 UEFA CUP:	1 Appearance

Mich D'AVRAY

Having progressed through the ranks at Portman Road, Mich D'Avray broke into the Ipswich Town first team in November 1979 when Bobby Robson handed him his debut in a 3-1 victory over Southampton at Portman Road.

Despite showing promise as a striker with an eye for goal, he remained on the fringes of the senior side for a number of years, although he did make a solitary appearance in the 1980/81 UEFA Cup run when he came off the bench in the second leg of the quarter-final tie against St-Étienne.

Mich began to figure regularly for Town throughout the 1980s and was capped by England twice at Under-21 level. Most notably he scored against Italy to help them into the finals of the 1984 UEFA European Under-21 Championships. His Town first-team career spanned over ten years before he joined Leicester City on loan early in the 1989/90 season, however, after only three appearances for the Foxes, he agreed a permanent move to Dutch club NEC Nijmegen.

In 1992, after only one season in Holland, Mich's playing career came to an end when he decided to hang up his boots and move into management, eventually going on to hold various posts in his native South Africa and also in Australia.

Robin TURNER

Robin Turner was one of a number of youngsters spotted by Ipswich Town scout John Carruthers while playing in local football in the Carlisle area. Robin signed for the Blues as an apprentice in 1971 and was a member of the club's youth team that lifted the FA Youth Cup two years later. After being capped by England at youth international level, he spent two years in the Ipswich Town reserves, before finally being handed his first-team debut in October 1975, when he came off the bench in a 1-0 defeat at Derby County.

First-team opportunities were limited, but he did make a major contribution to Town's 1978 FA Cup-winning campaign when he scored twice to earn them a 2-2 draw in the fifth round tie at Bristol Rovers. He also appeared in the semi-final victory over West Bromwich Albion, but unfortunately wasn't selected for the final against Arsenal at Wembley. Robin figured only once in Town's 1980/81 UEFA Cup run, coming off the bench late in the game against Bohemians in Prague, although he did almost score when his effort in the closing minutes was cleared off the line.

In all, Robin's career with Town lasted almost 14 years, but after a loan spell with Dutch club MVV Maastricht he joined Swansea City. There followed a brief spell with Colchester United before he retired from the game at the end of the 1985/86 season and moved into the teaching profession.

PLAYER PROFILE

DATE OF BIRTH:	18 February 1962
PLACE OF BIRTH:	Johannesburg, South Africa
IPSWICH TOWN:	255 Appearances · 48 Goals
1980/81 UEFA CUP:	1 Appearance

PLAYER PROFILE

DATE OF BIRTH:	10 September 1955
PLACE OF BIRTH:	Carlisle
IPSWICH TOWN:	62 Appearances · 6 Goals
1980/81 UEFA CUP:	1 Appearance

PAUL MARINER & JOHN WARK

By the time the triumphant party reached
the Town Hall in Cornhill, the whole town
square was a sea of blue and white with
dozens of supporters ignoring health and
safety by climbing lamp-posts and traffic
signs as well as scaling rooftops to ensure
they didn't miss out on what was probably
a once-in-a-lifetime experience.

BOBBY ROBSON

PAUL MARINER

Then Bobby Robson led his team out onto a specially erected balcony and one-by-one the players took a bow and hoisted the newly-won trophy to their adoring fans.

The biggest cheer came when Bobby Robson took centre stage and talked of his pride in taking Ipswich Town to the very pinnacle of European football, before finally assuring supporters that he would still be at the helm the following season having just turned down an approach from Sunderland and having opted not to apply for the manager's job at Manchester United.

RUSSELL OSMAN

UEFA CUP WINNERS 1980/81 40TH ANNIVERSARY
Roll of Honour

THANK YOU TO THE FOLLOWING FANS WHO PRE-ORDERED

Joshua Davies-Morris
Dennis Cyrille
Richard J Hart
Jonathan Beatton
David Read
Paul Bartolo
Chris Fleet
Phil Death
Peter and Annie Ross
Terry Fryatt
Justin Adams
Graham Adams
Renegade Statman
Tony Farrow
Neil Jenkins
Brian Evans
David Groom
Jonathan Bloomfield
Gary French
Barry Richardson
John Goode
John Edwards
Bob et Martine Porter
Mr Michael Sewell
Andrew Fayers
Matt Newman
David & Sharon Riddleston
Peter & Mandy Garner
Phil Bullard Blue Army!
Elizabeth Edwards
Nigel Richard Nunn
Neil Finbow
Kyle Roper
Robert Freeman
Malcolm Freeman
Joe-Tyla Butcher
Paul Butcher
Alan Taylor
Jay Button
Emerson Fairweather
George Turner
Andy Buckle
Matty Chaplin Stowmarket
Stefano
Roar Wulff Førde
Mike & Bob Martel 75-81
Jack Morris
Fiona Taylor

Frank Mooss
David ...Rfatownfan
Andrew McLellan
Glenn Sedgwick
Chris Ford
Barry Jessup
Izaak Morley Jessup
Darren Bull
Dale Osborne
Gordon Page
Rory
Jason Pegelow
Ken Blythe
Graham Turner
Mark McFarlane
Simon Tompkins
Christine Wood
James Wood
Barry Brough
Denise Hammond
Gary W Graves
Finn Prestney
Terry Alderson
Rod Gray
Russell Smith
David J. Allum
Christopher Harvey
Alan Mason
Stuart Grice
Paul Carter
Norman Skedge
Robert Skedge
Tim Skedge
Neil Peter Ross
Georgia Robbins
Chris Allum
Darryll P Walraven
Alan Seely
Adam Woody Woodmason
Adrian Le Cras
Justin Grimwood
Paul Goodchild
Nigel Chandler
Bob Lockhart
Martin & Suzie Burrows
Richard Pack
Douglas Grimwood
Yvonne Bell

Kevin Jackson
Tony Adams
Gary Chaplin
Keith Winter
David E Thomas
Andy De Vine
Neil Hartland
Richard Townsend
Lawrence John
Sean Lindsay
Peter John Beales
Andy Harling
John Bilverstone
Janet Lambert
Simon Francis
Paul Davies
Paul Gardner
Terry Walker
Stephen Curtis
Jon Tovell
Jean King
Robert Garrett
Alan Flewitt
Mark W Turner
Brian Andrews
David Andrews
Colin Kreidewolf
Richard Milner
Paul David Adams
Ben Hudson
Howard Beaumont
Alan Hynard
Carole Cross
Tim Raven
Geoff Cook
Craig Alexander
Paul Hart
Dennis Stannard
Tony Mayers
James Rochard
Phillip Gould
Charlie Brueton
Christopher Harris
Dominic Belisario
Richard Cragg
Jack Garnham
James Miller
Martin Wright

Holmesy
Neville Seager
Michael Sealey
Steven Brinkley
John Marazzi
Phil Bloom
Gillian D Church
George Whinney
James Ager
Bob Mills
Geoffrey Ferret Goymer
Fergal Johnson
Helen Cairns
Paul Brassey
Paul Pryke
John Rodas
Amanda Horley
Alex Gillingwater
Sam Chapman
Marc Humm
Jonny Josiah
Brian Sayers
Trevor Partridge
Andrew Reynolds
Neil Short
Peter Wood
Lee Robinson
Marc Borley
David Burgess
Graeme Brooke
Karl Fuller
Shaun Fuller
Simon Dines
Liam Hall
Ian Charles Flack
Stuart Whayman
Steve Mannell
Shaun Ellingham
Andrew Davies
Dale Downie
Richard Terrell
Dennis Mann
Steve Cross
Steven Vaughan
Jane Cowap
Colin & Stephen Pearson
John Mehen
Jacqueline Green

Philip Dickinson
Simon Nolloth
Simon Black
Roger Benstead
David Read
John Maynard
Stephen Butcher
Christopher Prime
Peter Welham
Adrian Judd
Nicholas Fenn
Gary Graves
Martyn Cardy
Andy Pearl
Niklas Moberg
Sara Gallop
Ray Long
Nigel Hood
Gerry Summons
Charlie Ramsell
Graham Almond
Chris Deal
Keith Abbott
Bernie Gaught
Steven Burgess
Mike Smart
Harry Nicholl
Charlie Nicholl
Mark Hitchcock
Derek Cook
Maria Keeble
Sarah Jane
Glenn Rees
Ashley Scrivener
Clive Mann
Chris & Wendy Hayes
Dan Gartlan
Richard Carter
Brian Blowers
Graham Colbourne
Bob Woods
Brian Roper
Tristan Woolfenden
Brian Peck
Trevor Last
Barry Allard
Alan Clarke
Martin Freeman

Paul Andrews
William E J Curtin
Derek Savory
Paul Whiting
Mary Carlill
Paul Wernham
Jayne Chapman
James Robbins
Ian McIntyre
Paul Jackson
Neil Prentice
Stephen Prentice
Marc Borley
Colin Coombs
C & B Brookwell
Mark Holdaway
Stuart Batte
George Perry
Tom Bright
Colin J Beer
Ivy Cutter
Derek Ivan Jarman
Tim Sparling
Paul Hedger
Phil Loy
Nigel Page
Reece Cox
James Wilmot
Terry Bailey
Peter Beesley
Alan Hawkes
Bill Hone
John Meekings
Michael Rowley
Paul Crouch
Neil Johnson
Alan Williams
Andy Dalziel
Mark Isaacs
James Minifie
Graham Downey
Stephen Downey
Brynley Bloomfield
John R Berry
Pauline Mann
Paul Miller
Andrew K Stevenson
Adrian Phillips

Chip Winstow
David Gray
Jeremy Cole
Roy Beggerow
John Monks
David Larke
Steve Hodge
Graham Nobes
Trevor C Ruffles
Peter Beer
Stuart Williams
Paul Baker
Gary McMorran
Martin Talbot
John S Bryan
Alistair Rattray
John M & Lisa A
Michael Alcock
Richard Green
Anne Green
Kuen-Wah Cheung
Oakley Groenhart
David Eaton
Mark Bennett
Richard Heath
Keith Nice
Ken Bullen
Adrian Tricker
Reg Tricker
Paul Edwards
Douglas Moye
Dale Hood
Zachary Meadows
Stefano Carniglia
Hans Peters - Holland
Peter Schou
Andy Thomson
David Riddleston
Martin Stonebridge
Richard Chenery
Peter G Sadler
Jackie Mortimer
Dan Fuell
Adrian Mills
Keith Stafford
Mark Smith
Steven Reynolds
Barry Calver

Paul Adams
Dave Owen
Dan Ford
Geoff Frost
Gerry Moyes
Carol & Steve
Paul Freak
Stu Chisholm
Eric Oram
Colin Taylor
Mark Taylor
Carolyn Stannard
Matthew Try
Adrian 'Fred' Fincham
Brian Boar
Stephen Fewkes
Beryl Vincent
Amanda Olle
Tom Allen
Paul Brinkley
Brian Rayner
Kim Salmon
Malcolm Sanders
Duncan Sheekey
Terry Bates
Laurie Miles
Paul Atkinson
Aiden & Jacob Annone
Tim Wilkins
Andrew Button
Dean Roseman
Bill Arbin
Marc Emmerson
Ian Dessent
John Bowers
Paul Peachey
Russell Simpson
Colin Greening
Alan Cattermole
Barry Willingham
Dean Willingham
Ian Baylis
Ben Ramsey
Arthur Pope
Matthew Wilson
Maurice Ashton
Jason Paul Smith
Allez les Bleus!
Peter Tweed
Mark Dowling
Kathleen M M Vidal
Alan Turner
Mark Riches
Stephen Tuckwell
Crumpton Clarke
Mark Prigg

Jeff Bennett
Ian Daldry
Matthew Steward
Julian Abigail
Robert Reeves
Ray Whitehand
Michael Gabbey
Simon Sheppard
Steve Bennington
Steve Drake
Tony Manning
Ian Dorling
Steve Thomson
Gerald West
Karen West
Melvin Coe
Chris Barker
Seán Murphy
Graeme Peck
Colin Dawson
Teddy Saunders
Brian Haward
Paul Pearson
Matthew Noble
Mark Paternoster
Alex Hall
Mark Ramsay
Simon Taylor
John Farthing
Paul Humphreys
Graham Blackburn
Jon Banger
Tirlochan Singh Lovlee
Andrew Baxter
Andrew John Salmon
Steve Ager
Gary Ager
Stuart Owen Watkinson
Stephen Philpot
Colin Bush
Philip Lown
Paul Piney Herring
Richie Munson
John Miller
Stephen Giddings
James Barker
Karen Smith
Dale Phillips
Ken Rouse
Nigel Dade
Conrad Staff
Tony "Pop" Pyther
Phil Waites
Stephen Lake
Carlton Matthew
Ian

Simon Holley
Maxwell Constantinou
Paul Sheehan
Peter Mahoney
Peter Sparrow
Kelvin Sherman
Paul Cook
Kenneth Grimwood
Scott Bishop
David 'Wink' Peachey
Nick Bruce
Matthew Moore
Geoff Horrex
Andrew Horrex
Amy Downes
Steve Carter
Robin Wright
Simon Aldred
Richard Snape
Matthew Clarke
Stephen Wade
Michael O'Sullivan
Joseph Barrow
Heather Webb
Debra Plunkett
Andy Miller
Max Pitchford
Eddie Green
John Michael Cook
Paul Herring
Jamie Weddell
Matt Plant
Ian Hall
Chris Turton
Jasper 'Jaspman' Conrad
Paul Curtis
Darren Judd
Francis Thijssen Law
Ray Kemp
Tom Roden
Colin Westgate
Russell Lomax
Ian Brendish
Thomas Wadsworth
Chris Rose
Michael Godfrey
Nick Tudor
Shaun Tracey
Gerry James Ruffles
Oriel Simpson
Welsh Tractor Girl
Steve Morley
Roger Tulley
Ken Browne
Martin L
Michael Drew

Gerald Scruby
David Sheppard
Christopher Marshall
Anita Garwood
Morgan Cook
Adrian Cooper
Jean Norman
Ian Taylor
Gerald Olley
Peter Basford
Charlie & Wendy Clarke
Geoff Swain
Badger
Andrew Barber
Cooper Flurrie
Gareth Reynolds
Alex Henderson
Keith Thompson
Andy Abrahams
Raymond Maskell
Clive Maskell
Sandra Hines
Nick W Fitch
Brian P Martin
Geoffrey Bingham
Shaun J Cobbold
Ian Gale
Don Dykstra
Brian Desmond
Dave Kreamer
Colin Bones
Andrew Harris
Philip Harris
Grandad Roy
Adrian Kite
Karl Malone
Jonathan Presland
Ian Morgan
Gary Wright
Benjamin Moore
Steven Farthing
David Beadle
Michael Oliver
Tim Cracknell
Eric Cox
Jeff Norman
Chris Bere
Richard Monks
Phil Taylor BA
David Dickinson
Ace Bugg
Kevin Higham
David Arnott
Martin Page
Paul Lightfoot
Peter Enguell

John Mainprize
Roger Porter
Vernon Forsdyke
Lee Forsdyke
Gordon Garnham
Mike King
Grahame Cryer
Phil Hanks
Clive Gardiner
Michael & James Sleet
Michael Edwards
Sandra Bartlett
Richard Lord
Peter Lord
Nick Goddard
Jack Carpenter
Jacqueline Green
John Long
Stuart Gibbs
Andrew Ling
Adrian Fabri
Andrew Chenery
Susan Bumstead
Peter Matthews
Matthew Becker
Brett Mansell
Geoff Sykes
Andrew Thomas
Mark Wadeson Berry
George Plowman
Nick Murton
Kevin Clarke
Paul Austin
Terry Green
Simon Drake
Rory Beer
Keith Banthorp
David Rayner
Tony Ferrell
Ian Galloway
Scott Robertson
Patrick Simpson
Charlie Clark
Robin Morley
Paul Hunt
Mark Dearlove
Peter Franklin
Richard Woodward
Raymond Alderton
Callum Duncan
Steve Lewis
Kevin Wilson
Nigel Ford
James Holden
Michael Bicker
Steve Waters

Daniel Palmer
Tim Beecroft
Pete Teevan
Jez
Justin Aldis
John Monks
Robert Avis
John Butcher in Harrow
Stephen Cook
Tom Anderson
Ray Cooper
David Hughes
Warren Boore
George Hayter
Adrian Sherman
Karl Brooks
Robert Mutimer
Iain Jack
Phil Mays
Andy Grimsey
Simon Thorpe
Chris Salmond
Fred Larke 1917-1984
Andrew Bradley
Paul Bradley
Philip Barbrook
Stuart Barbrook
Nick Smith
James Smith
Kieron Smith
Matt Donaldson
Bjarne Krarup Wulff
Paul Sloane
Danny Connolly
Stuart Spreadbridge
Ken Albon
Richard Leeks
Raymond James Parker
Ken Newman
Stephen Fayers
Glyn Evans
Trevor Mann
Joe Fairs
Ken Daynes
Ewan Livingston
Calum Livingston
Duncan Addison
Graham Gunn
Mervyn Johnston
Richard Gous
Andrew Harrison
Richard Way
Chris Robinson
Ian Longman
Roger Knights
Steven Greenwood

Peter Shelcot
Ray Witton
Jimmy H Gill
Andrew Dowse
Charlie Long
Richard Burke
Gary Barley
James Eadie
Freddie Maxted
Shirli Drummond
Andrew Clare
Ian & Averil Lockwood
Simon Wilcox
Callum Lloyd
Paul Allen
Michael Kettle
Daniel Mayo
Rob Burns
Thomas Block
Julie Tunney
Mark Rattle
Roy Unwin
Jason Cattermole
David Fulker
Andy Martin
Josh Muir
Gareth J Edwards
Tim O'Leary
Julian Clubb
Mark A. Haynes
J. Casey
Kevin Butcher
Paul Garnham
Gary Drew
Big Phil
Michael Hicks
Mr Bowman
Ralph Robinson
Hayden Ransome
Howard Garnham
Simon Emerson
Billy Robinson
Dizzy Debs
Stephen Sheldrake
Nick Rawlings
Dave Brown-Sawyer
Geoffrey
Chinery
Dad
Suzanne
Malcolm
James
Jamie
Steve

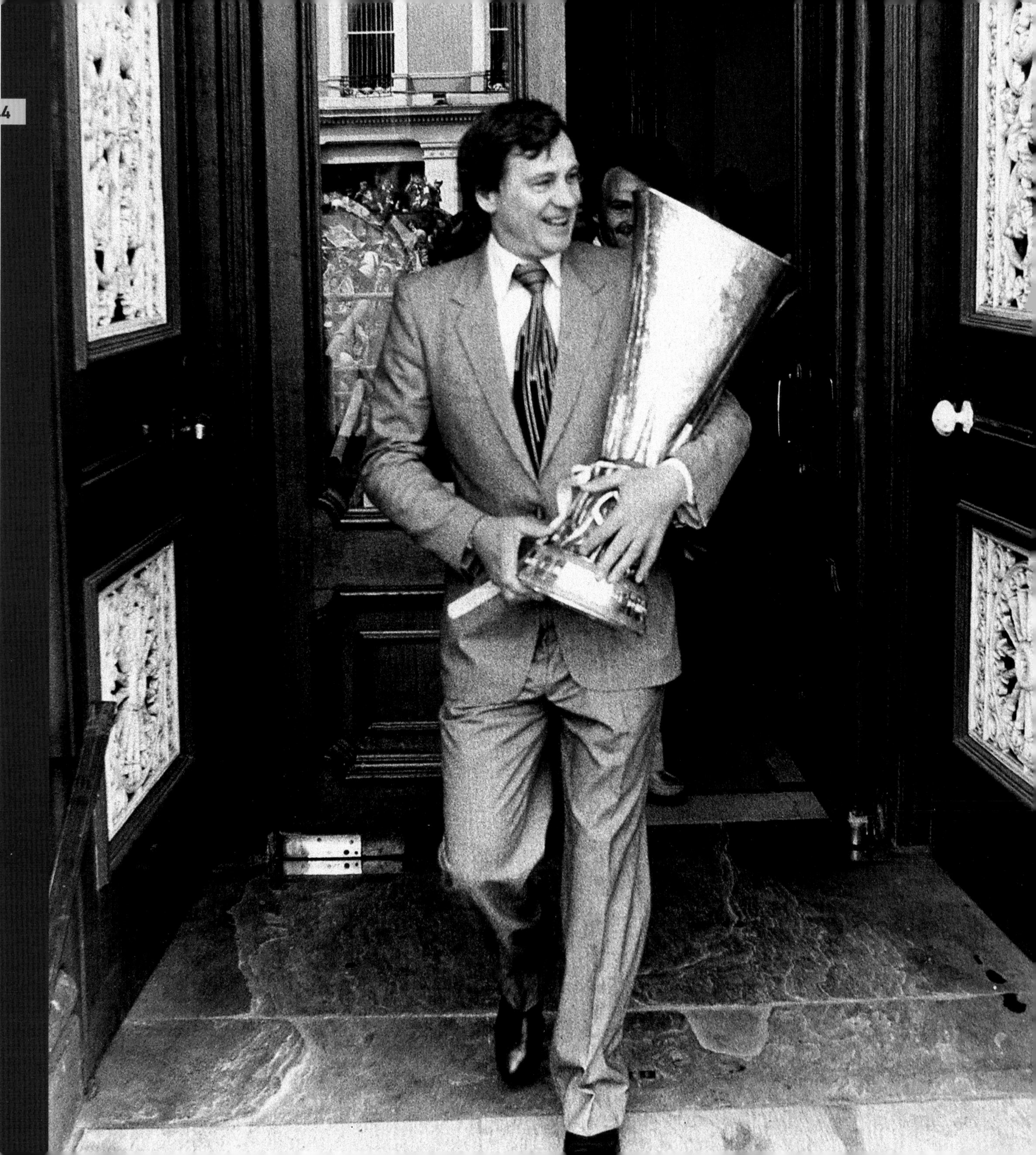